My First
Learn To Write
Activity Workbook

By

DADAM *trace*©

DADAM*trace*©

Copyright © 2020 by DADAMtrace ©

This book belongs to :

....

....

Alphabet Letters A-Z   **DADAM**_trace_ ©

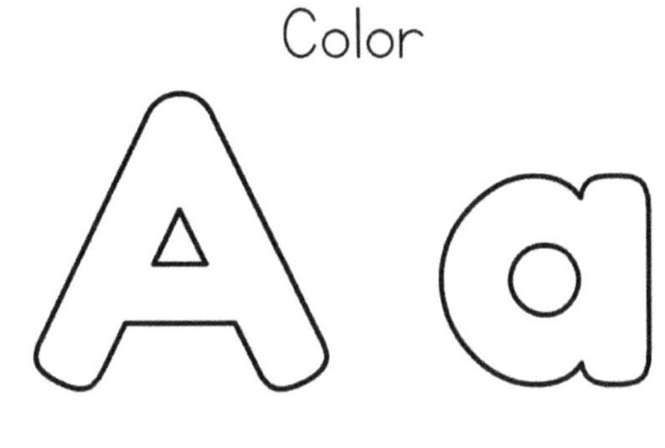

Color

Color

Apple

Circle it

b A a i A a C q
H a E A K a Z a
A a N o a I q d

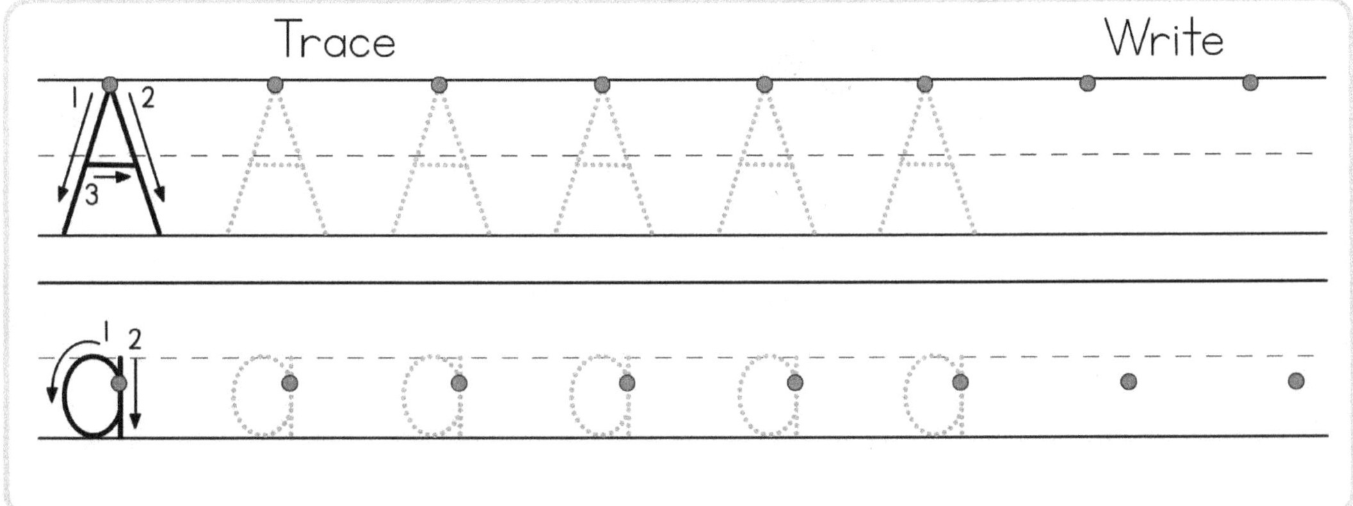

A - B - C -
- D - E - F -
- G - H - I -

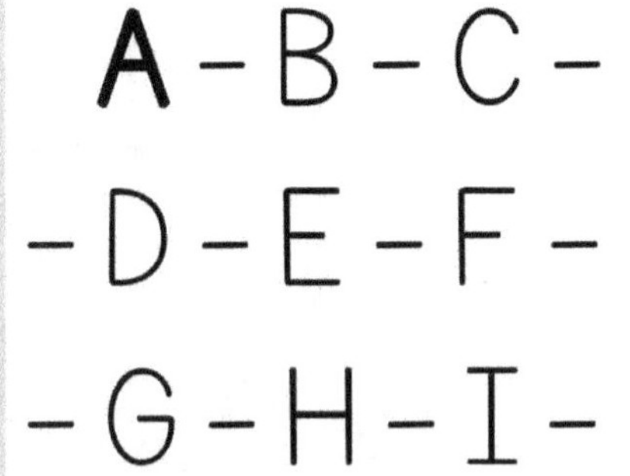

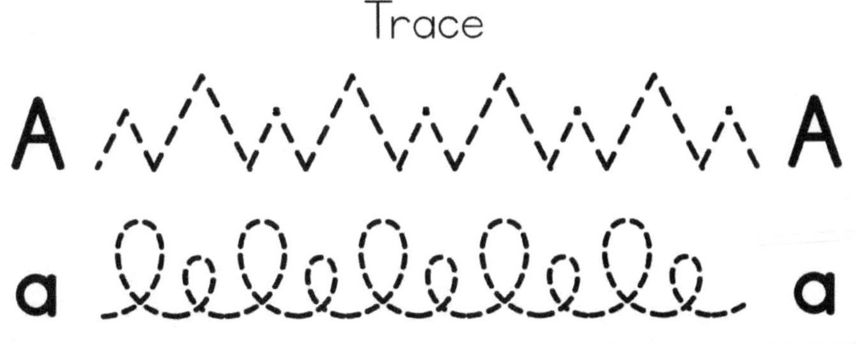

Alphabet Letters A-Z

Color

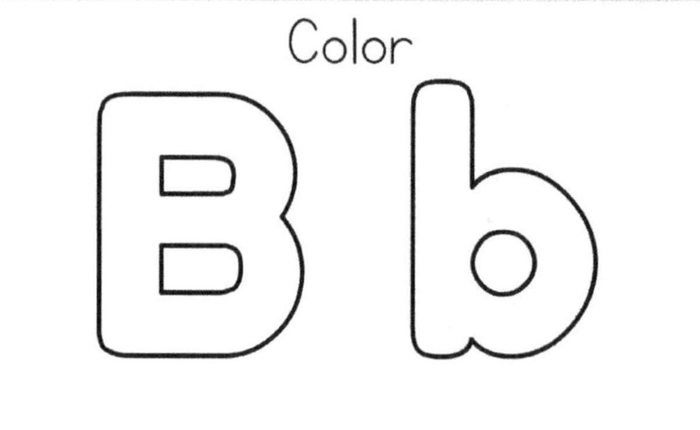

Color

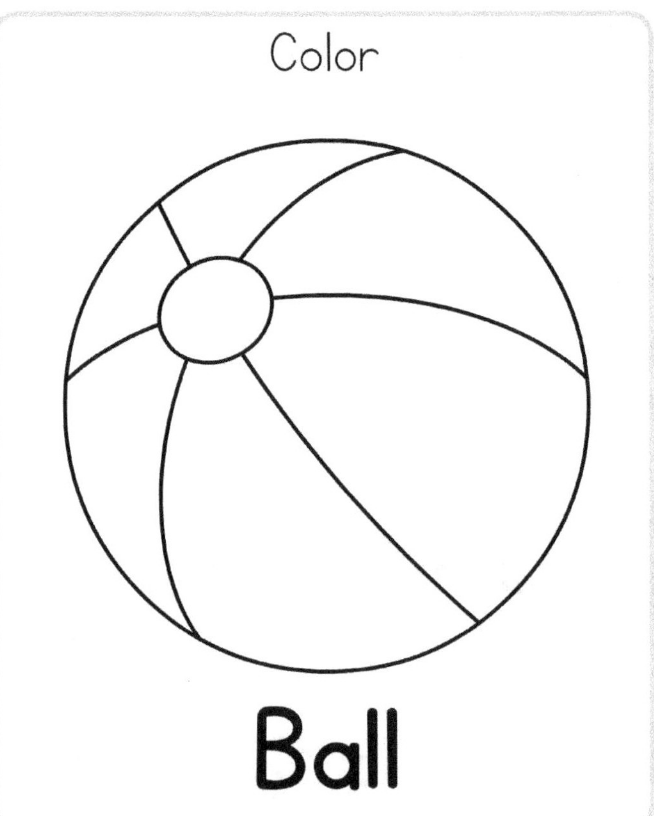

Ball

Circle it

a b R d P p B a
B p R b c B d b
b B c B a q b g

Trace   Write

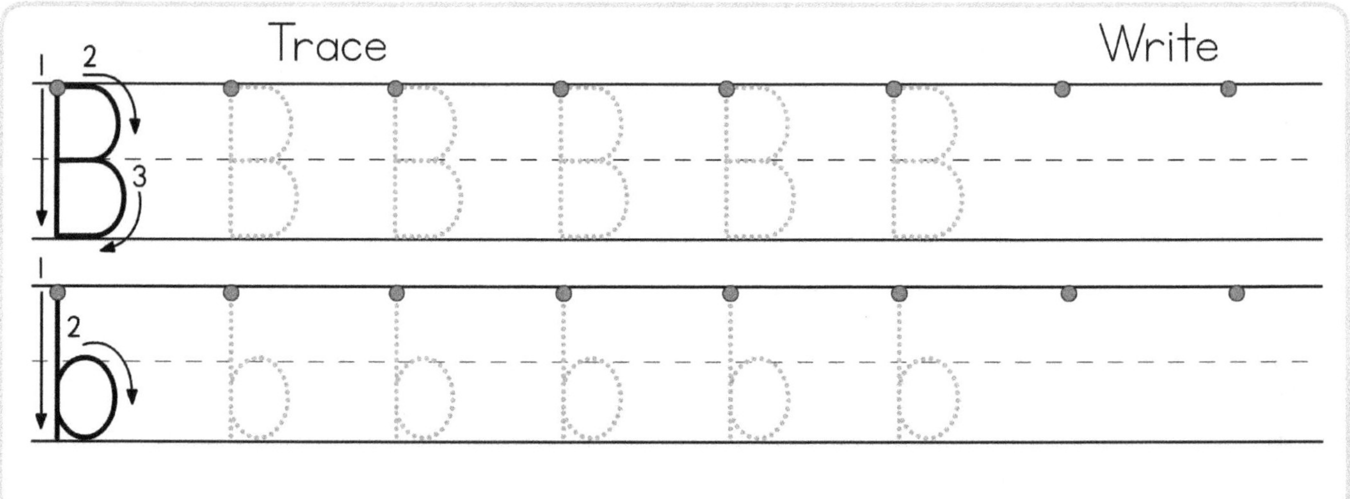

A - B - C -
- D - E - F -
- G - H - I -

Trace

B   B
b   b

Alphabet Letters A-Z

Color

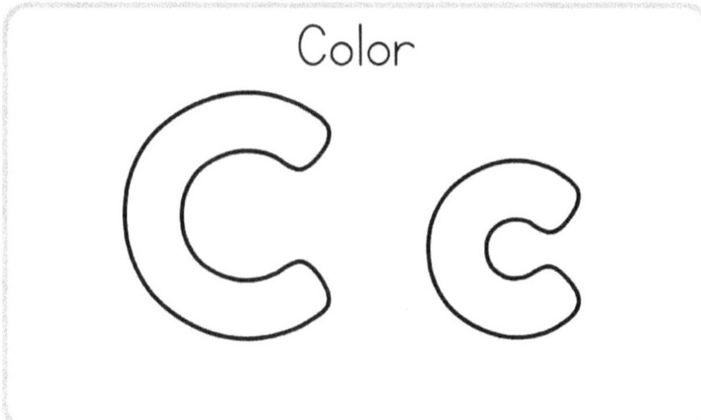

Circle it

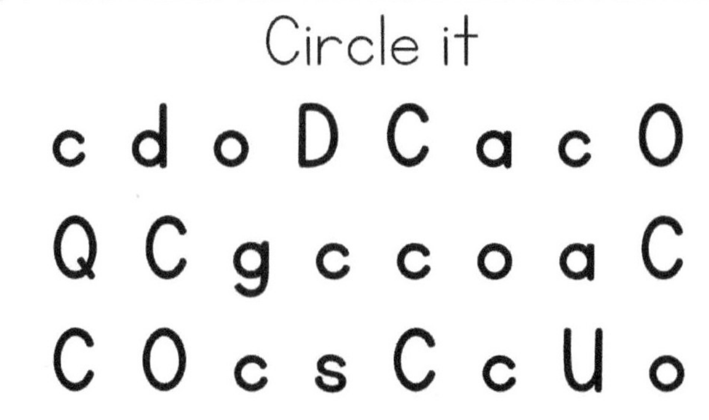

Color

Cat

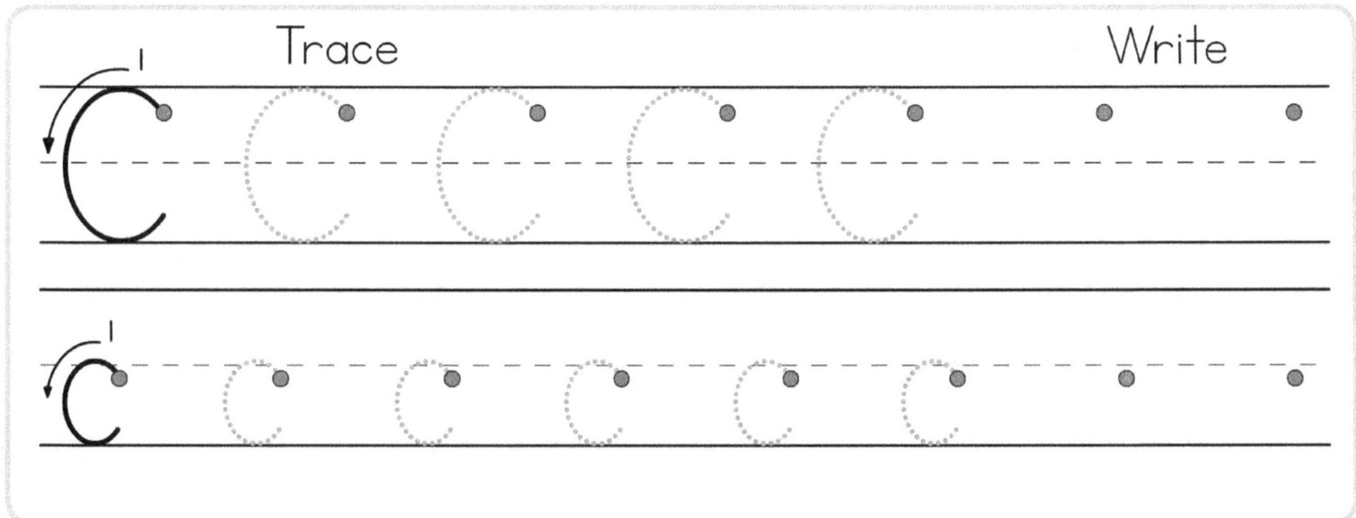

A - B - C -
-D - E - F -
-G - H - I -

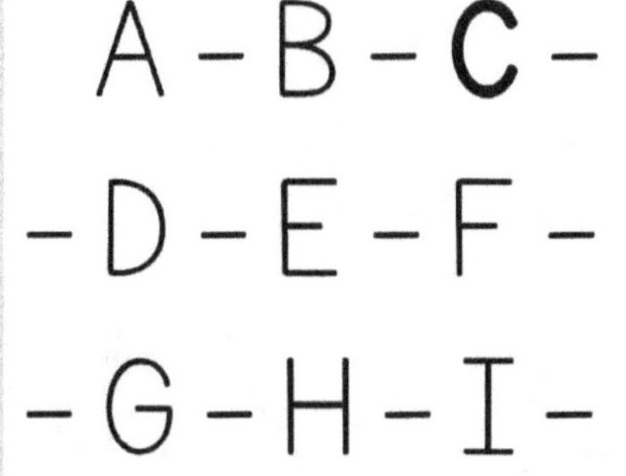

Trace

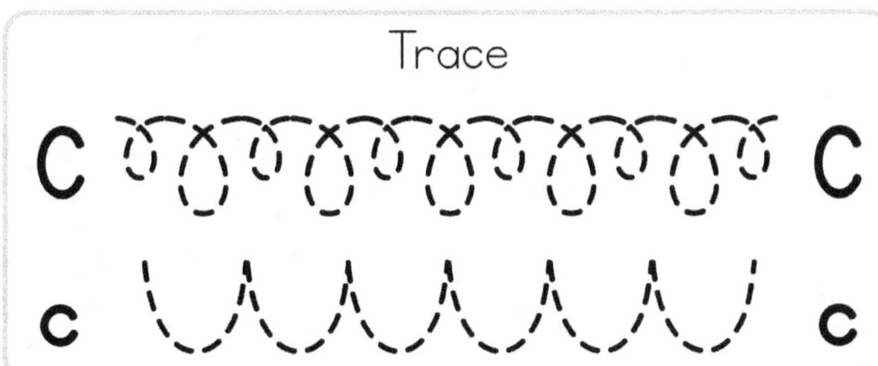

Alphabet Letters A-Z

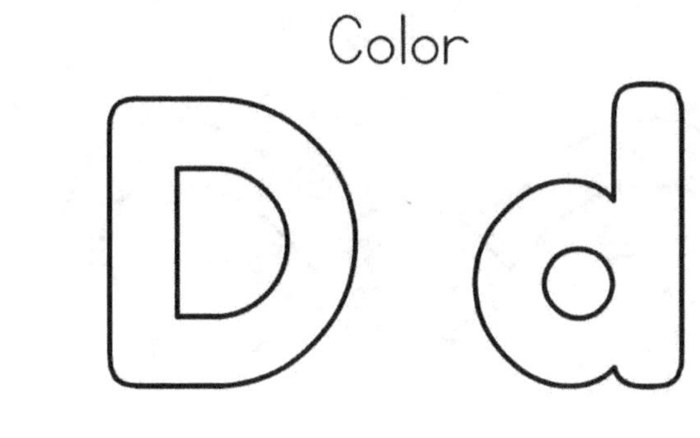

Color

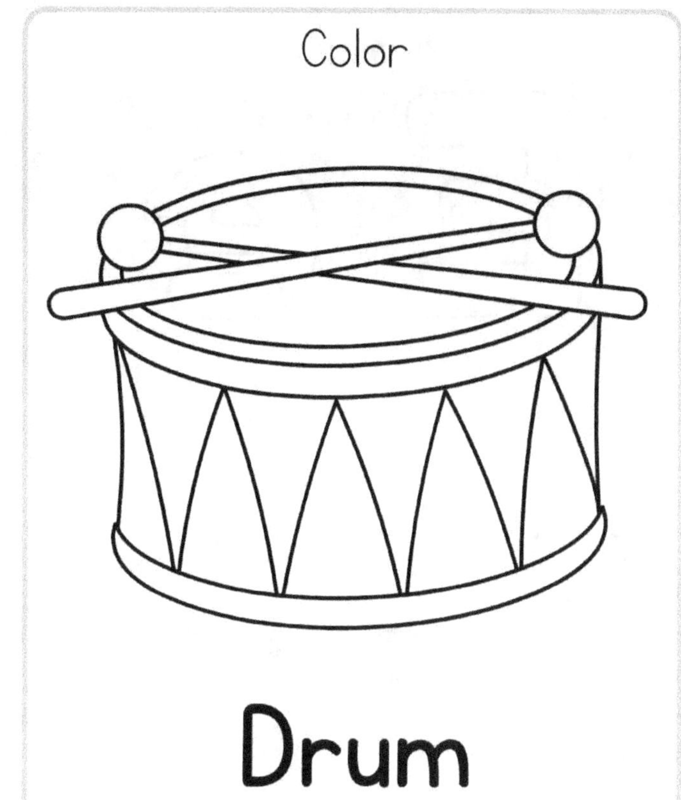

Color

Drum

Circle it

O d b p D B d b
d O p D a D q d
q d O D d p O D

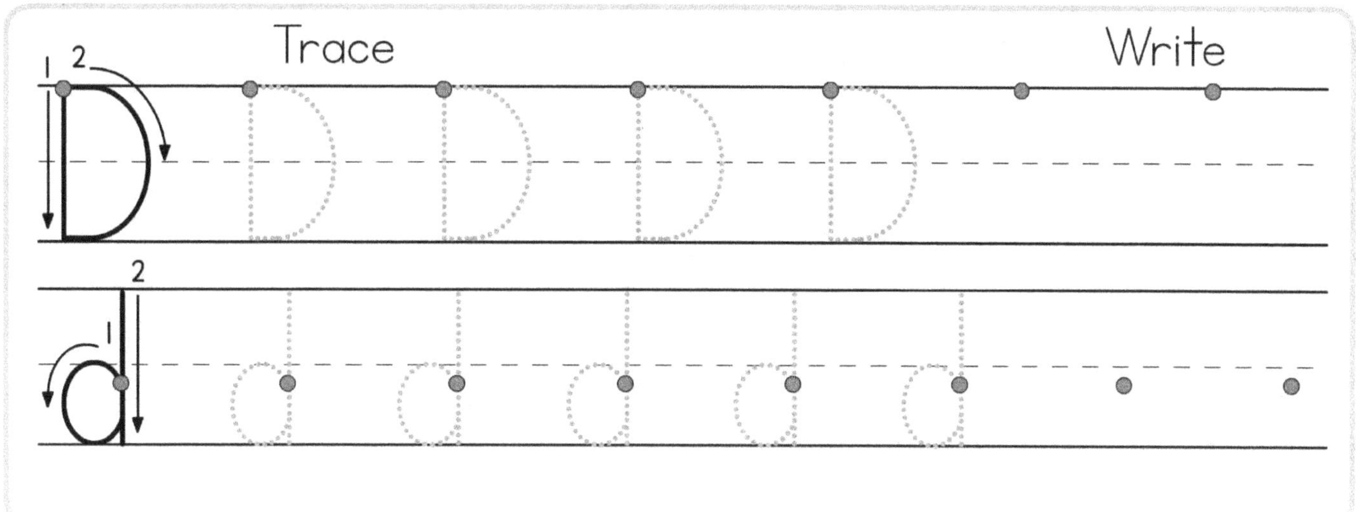

Trace

Write

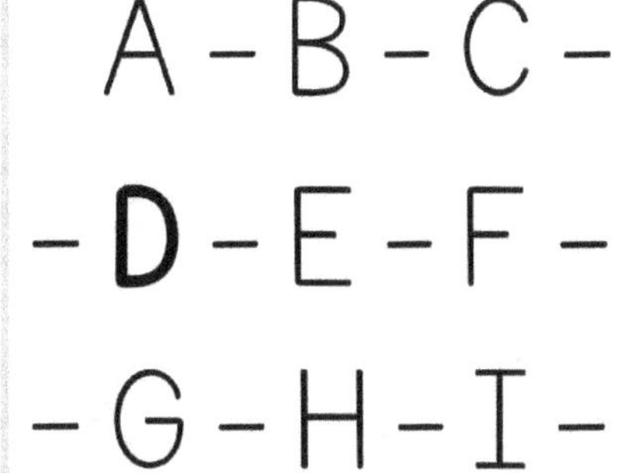

A - B - C -
- D - E - F -
- G - H - I -

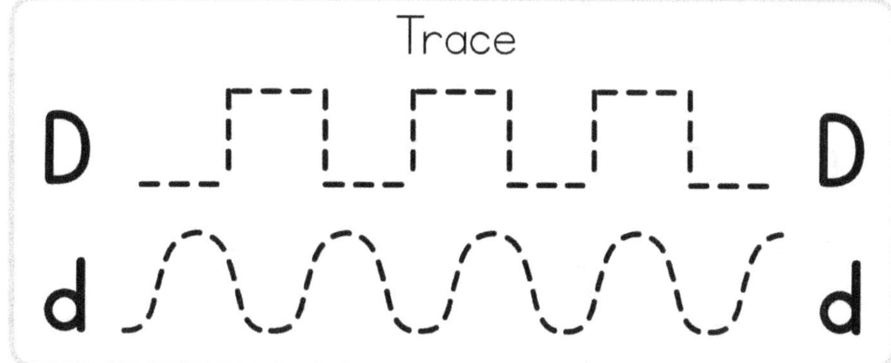

Trace

D D

d d

Alphabet Letters A-Z

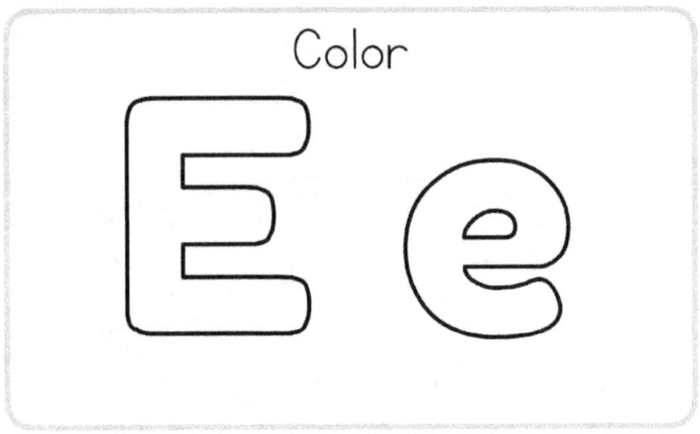

Circle it

E F e s o E H e
B e e E s F E o
e F o E E H e s

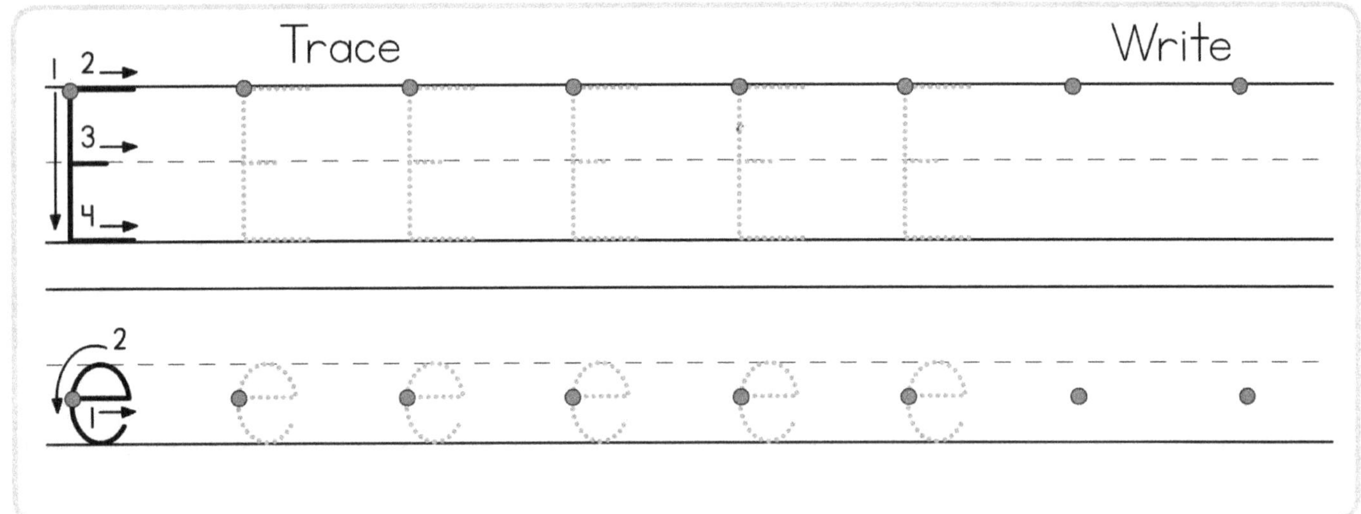

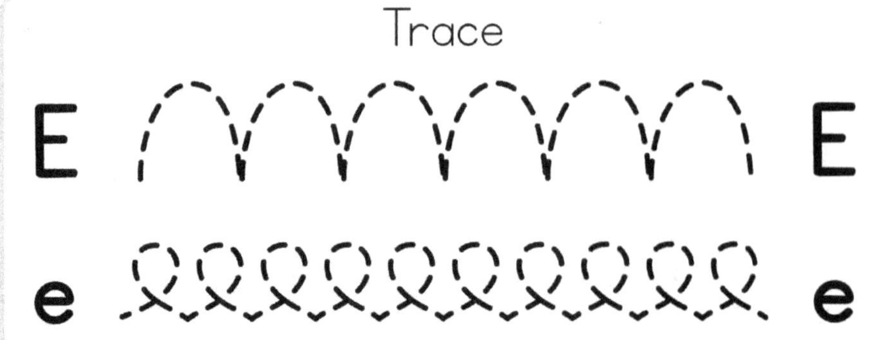

Alphabet Letters A-Z

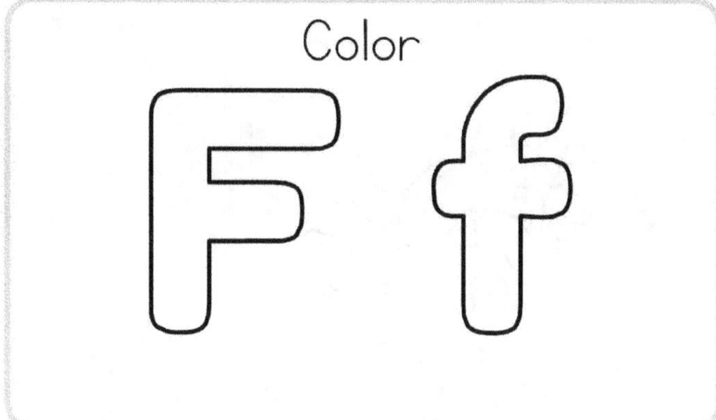

Circle it

f E F t h f H F
t f H F k h F F
f f E h F t H f

Trace / Write

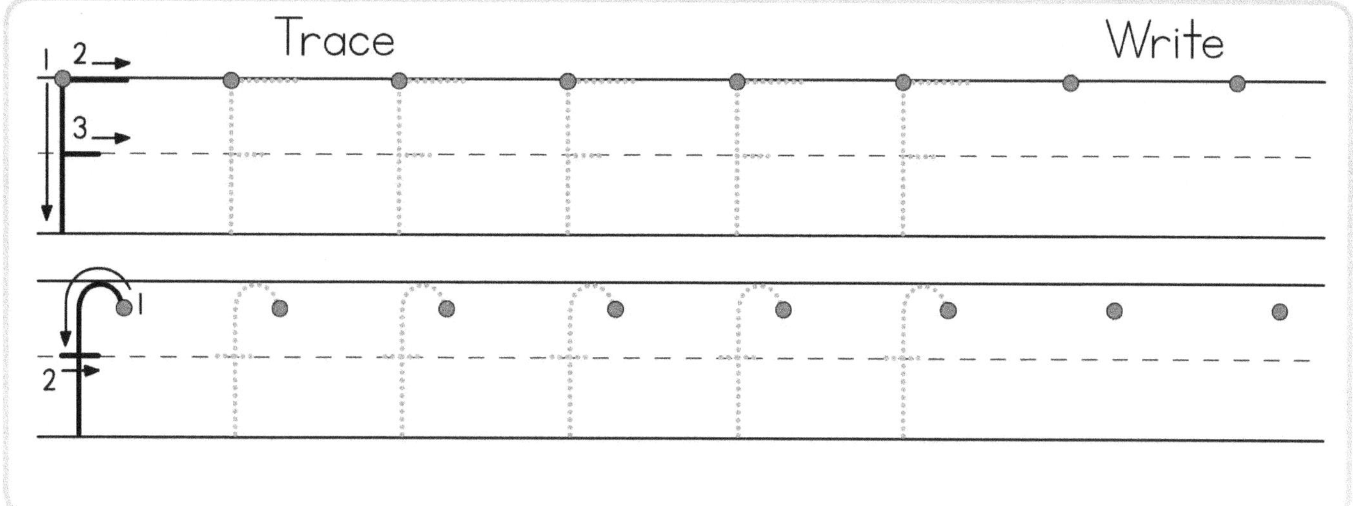

A - B - C -
-D - E - F -
-G - H - I -

Trace

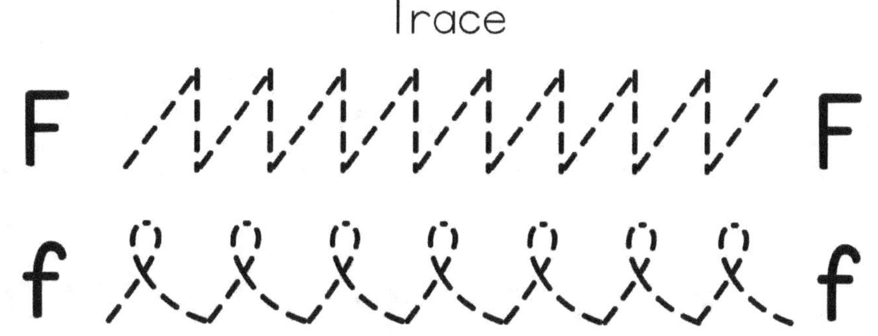

Alphabet Letters A-Z

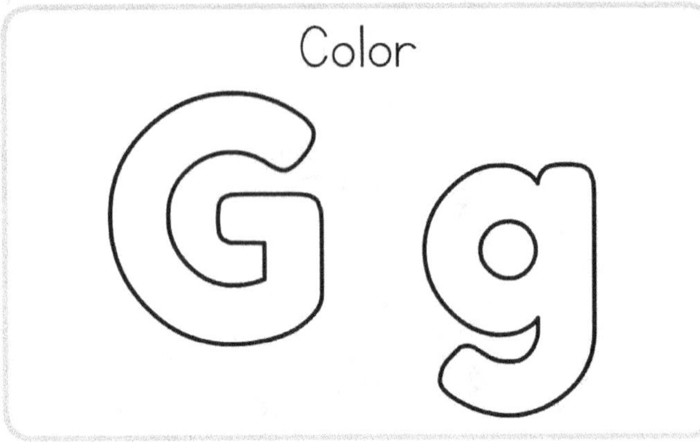

Circle it

q G p g O q g G
O g C G G q g g
g G q C p g C Q

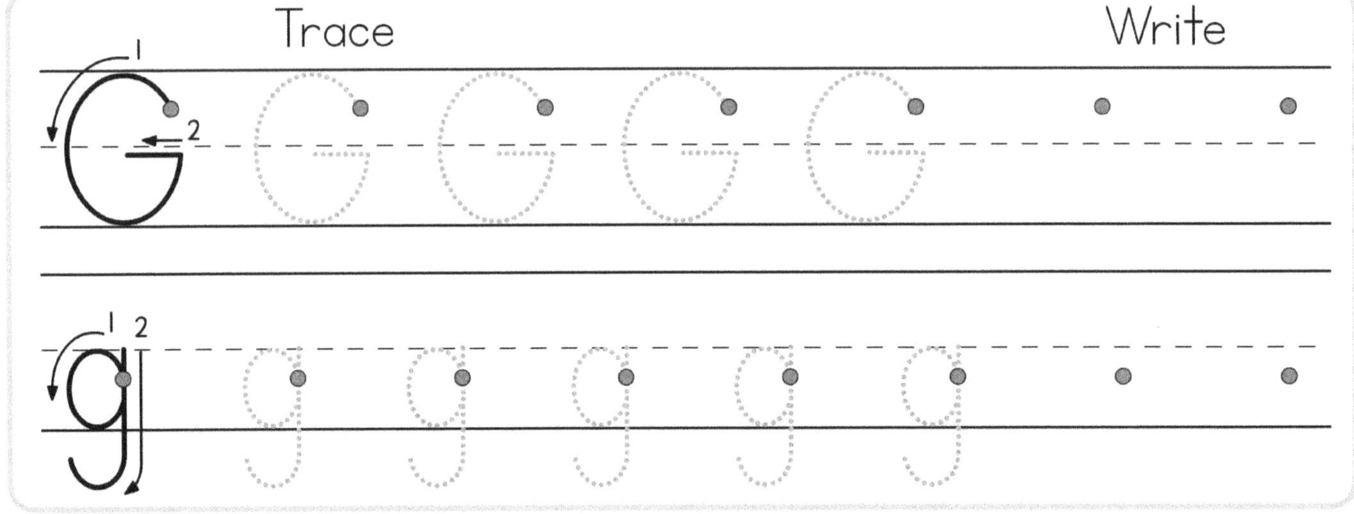

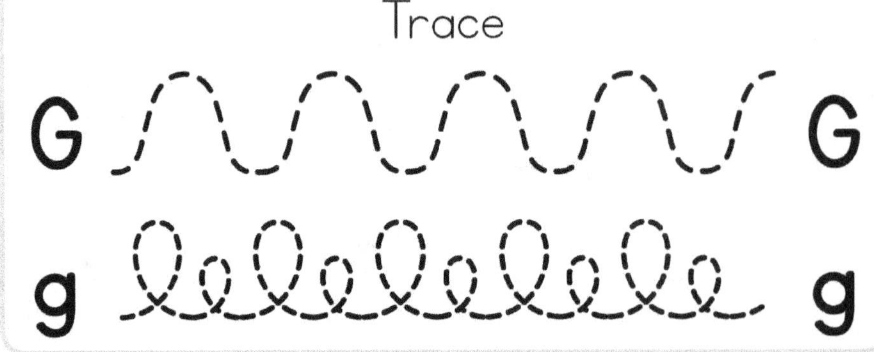

Alphabet Letters A-Z

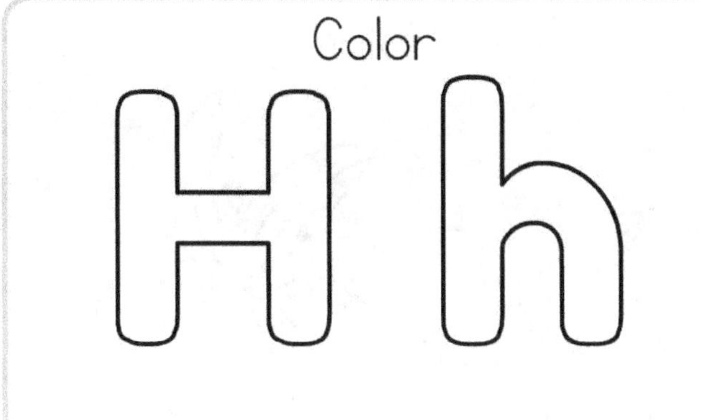

Circle it

h H K h n H N h
k h N H E h n H
H h E k h n H N

Trace   Write

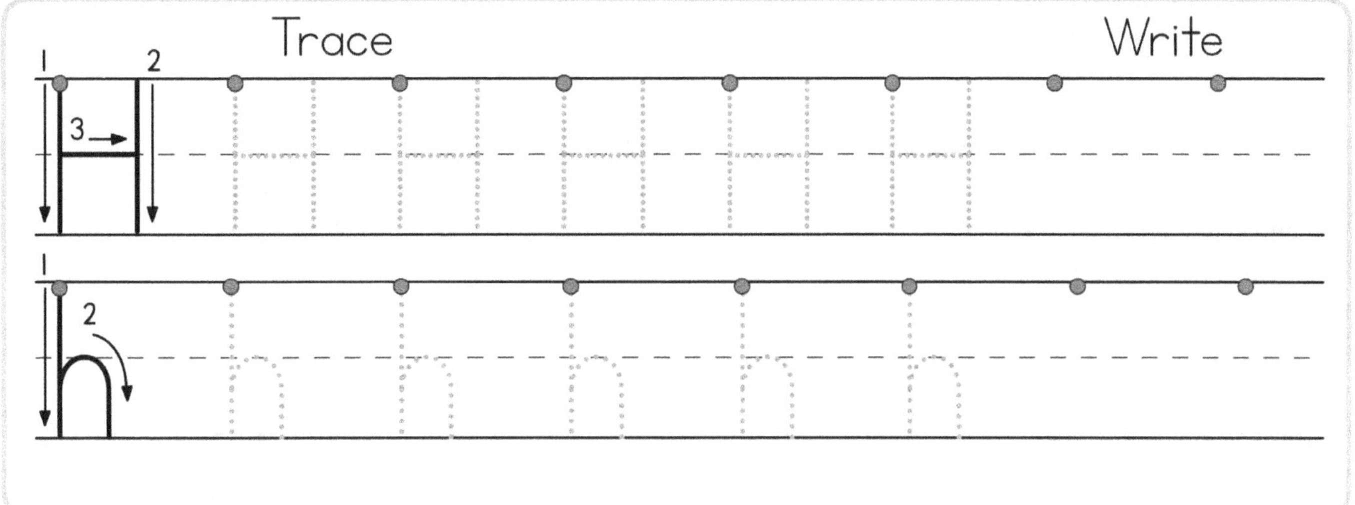

-D-E-F-

-G-H-I-

-J-K-L-

Trace

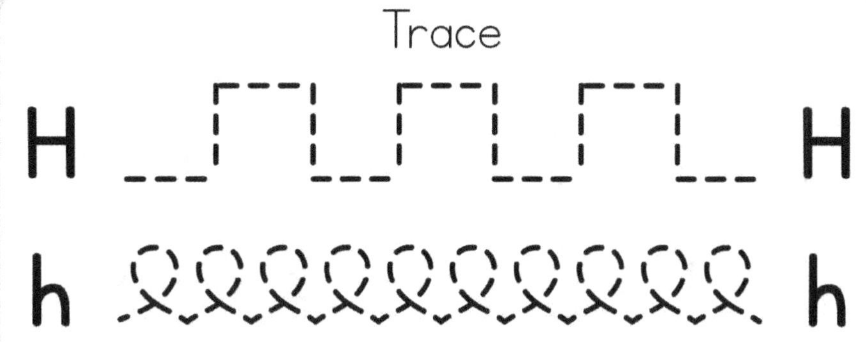

Alphabet Letters A-Z

Color

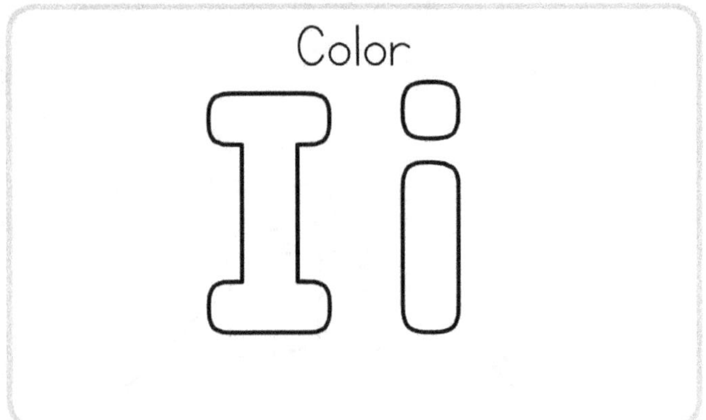

Color

Island

Circle it

I i L T I L i T
i L I T I L i I
L I i t i I T t

Trace   Write

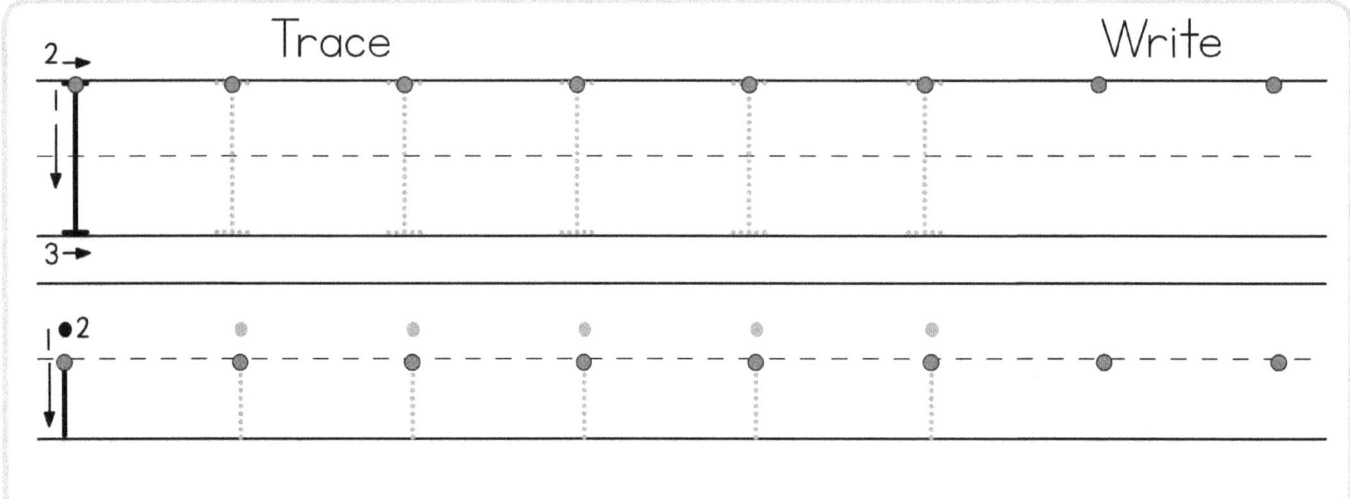

-D- E- F-
-G- H- I-
-J- K- L-

Trace

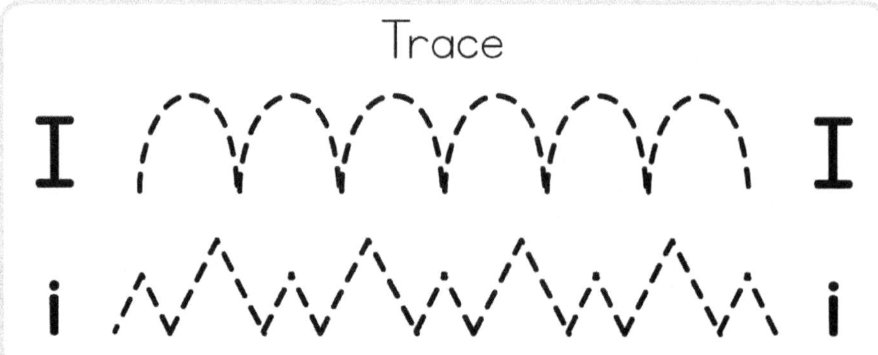

Alphabet Letters A-Z

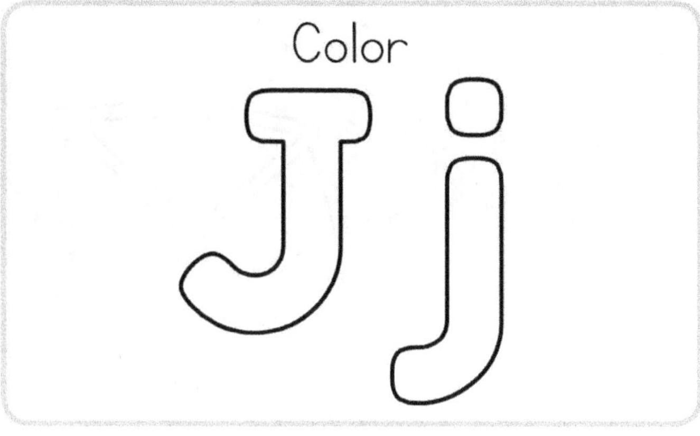

Color

Color

Jam

Circle it

j J T j T L j t

J t T j J j T L

T J T j L t J j

Trace   Write

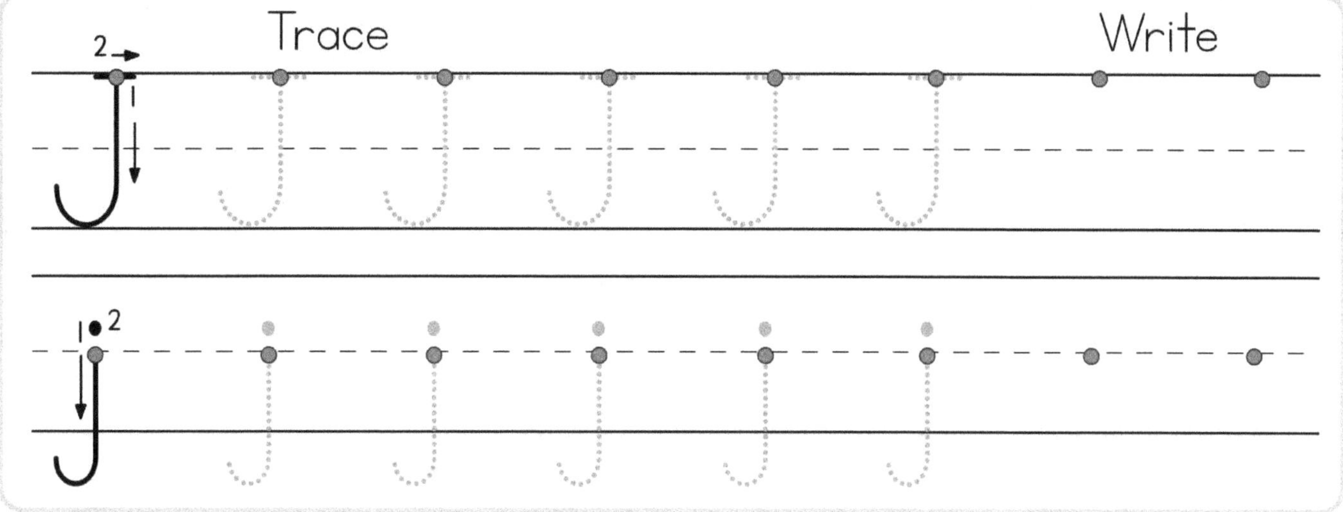

-G-H-I-
-J-K-L-
-M-N-O-

Trace

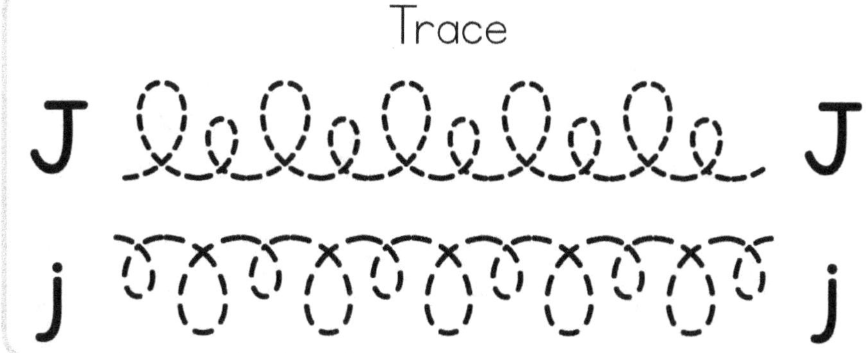

Alphabet Letters A-Z

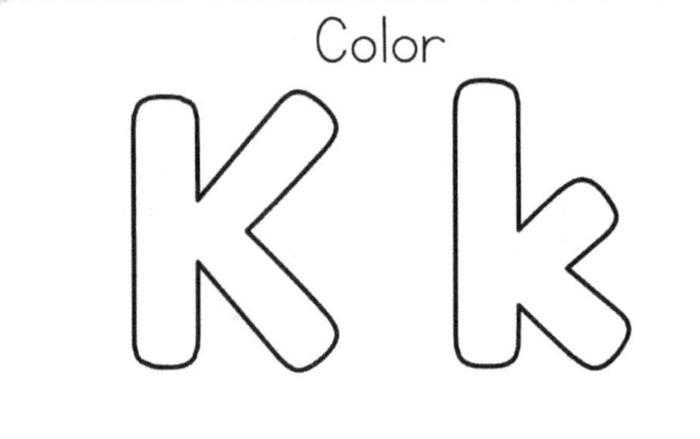

Circle it

k K h k F x K X
F k x K k K h E
k X K F k h x K

Trace · Write

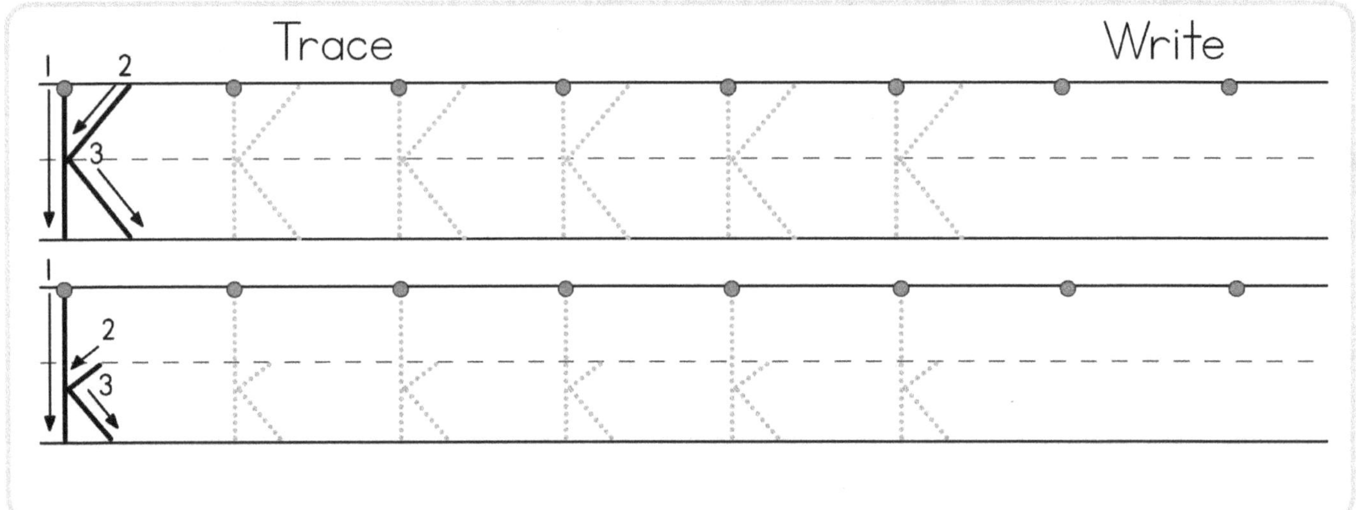

-G-H-I-
-J-K-L-
-M-N-O-

Trace

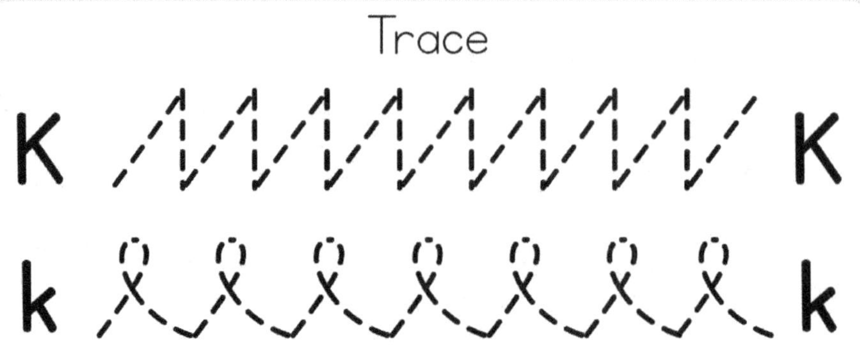

Alphabet Letters A-Z

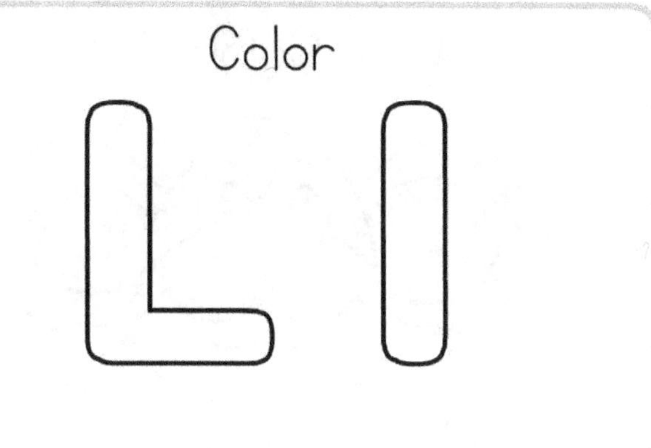

Circle it

L F l i H L I J

I L i V L t l j

F j l H j L I L

Trace   Write

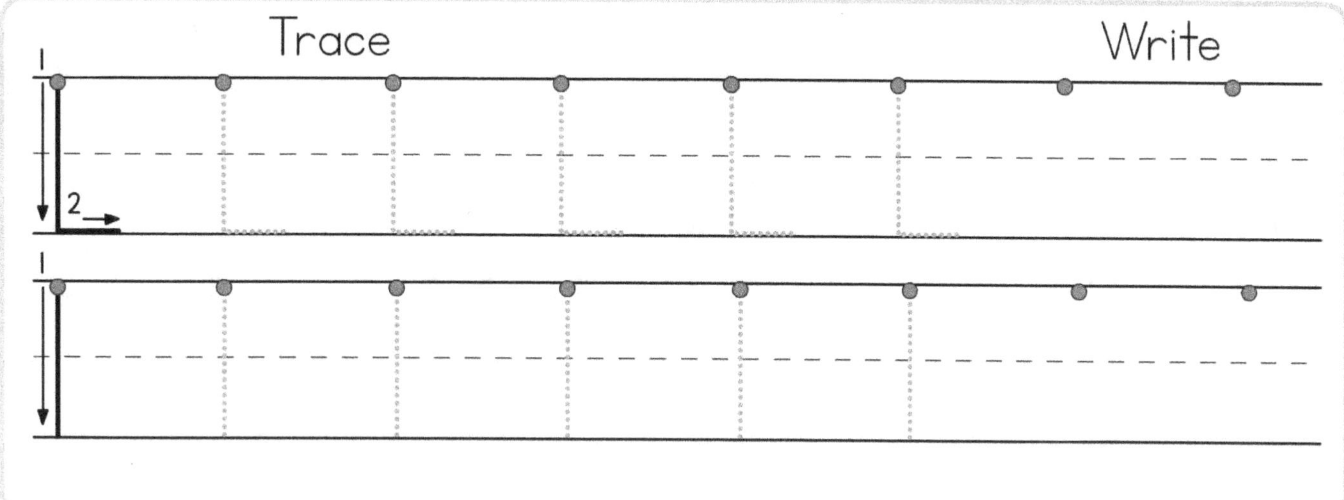

- G - H - I -
- J - K - L -
- M - N - O -

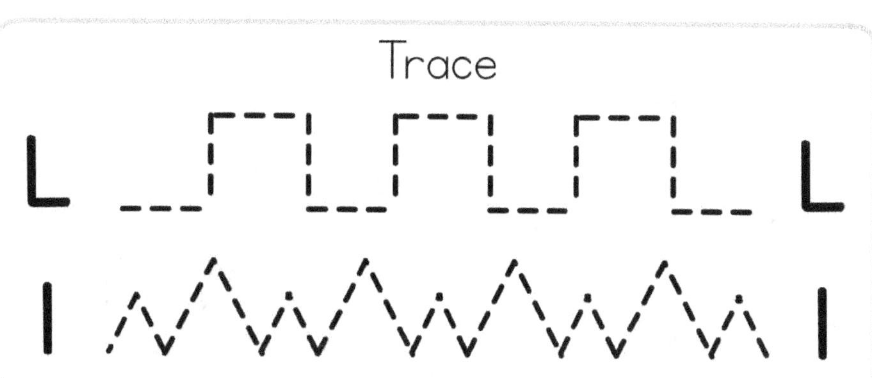

Alphabet Letters A-Z

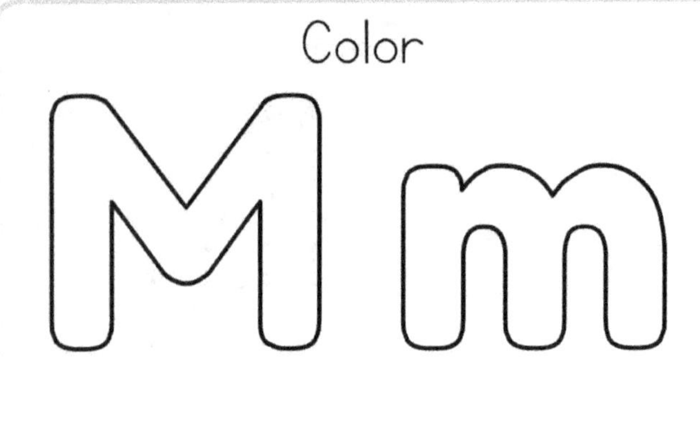

Circle it

m n M N m M w
m M w N W n m
N m W M n M m

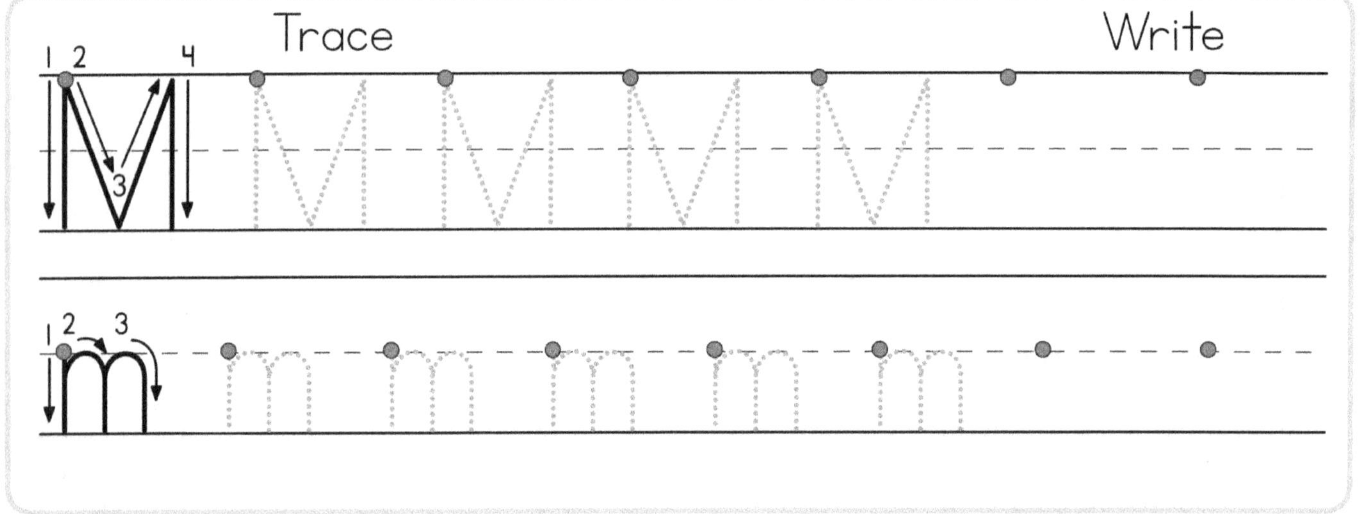

-J-K-L-
-M-N-O-
-P-Q-R-

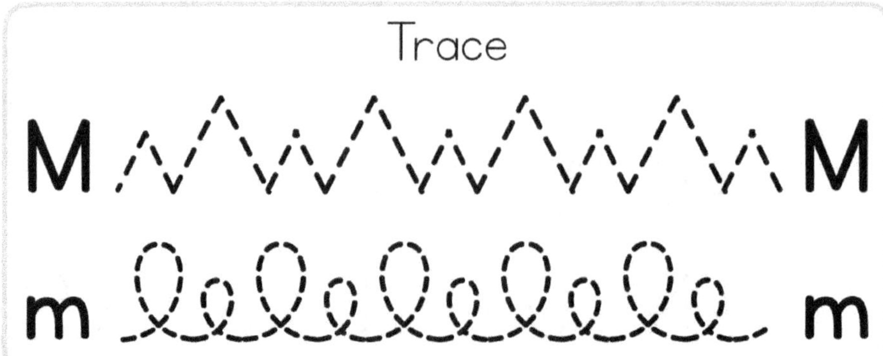

Alphabet Letters A-Z

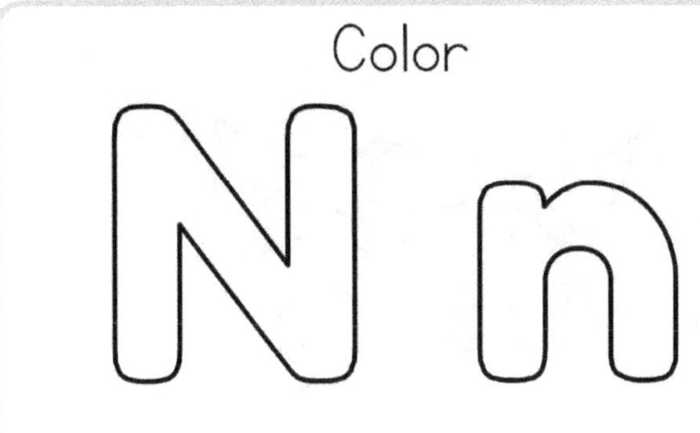

Circle it

M n h N H n N u

n N u h H n N h

N h n M N n u H

Trace Write

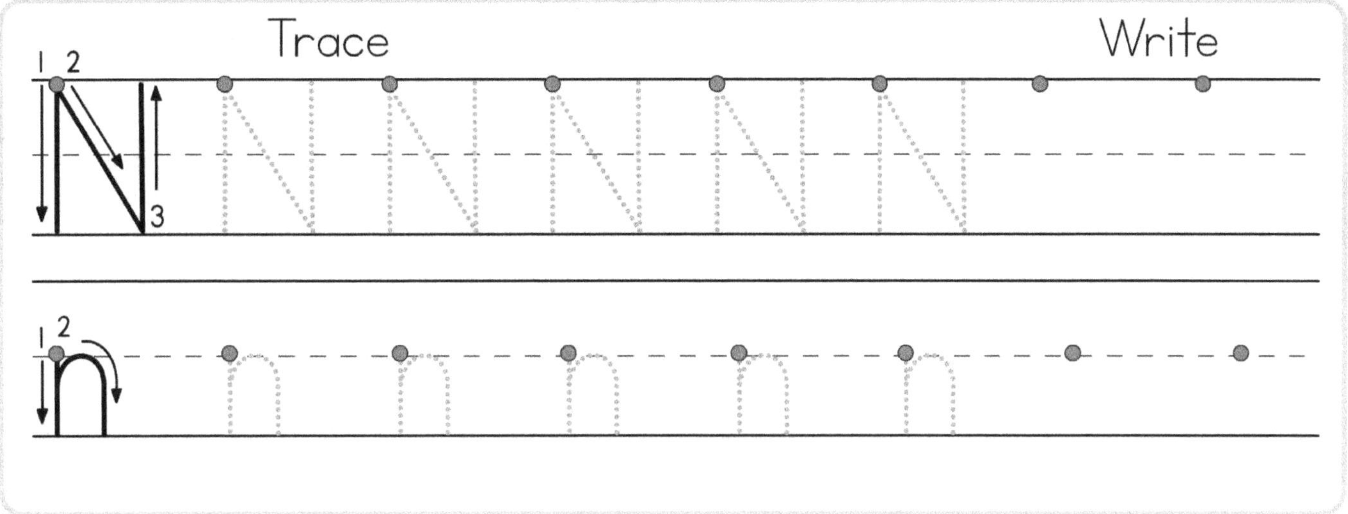

-J - K - L -

-M - N - O -

-P - Q - R -

Trace

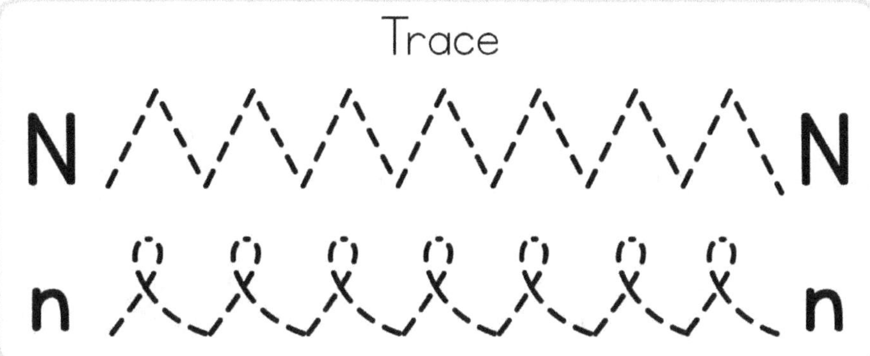

Alphabet Letters A-Z

Color

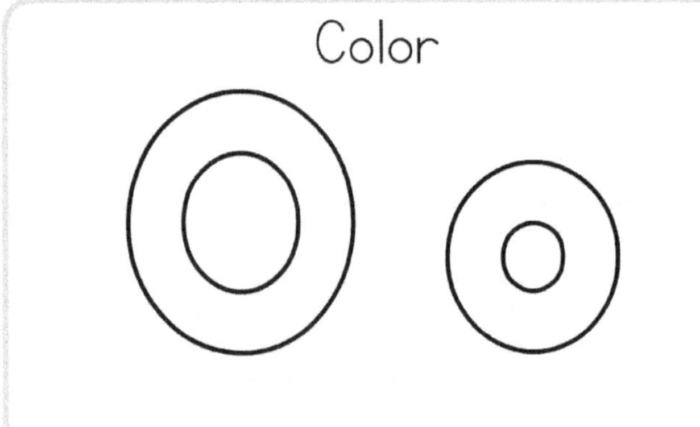

Circle it

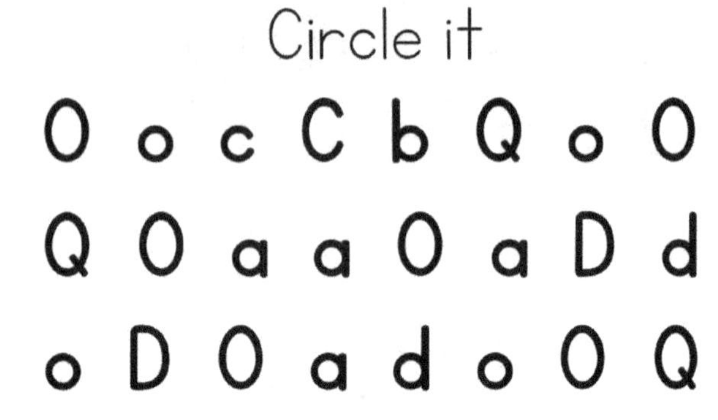

Color

Owl

Trace   Write

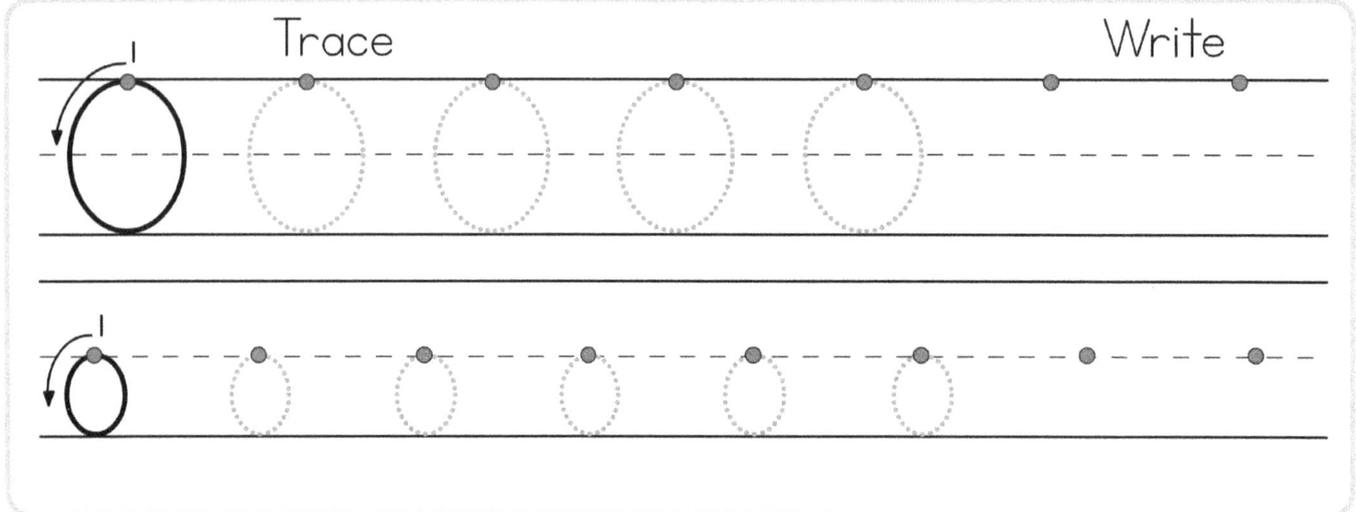

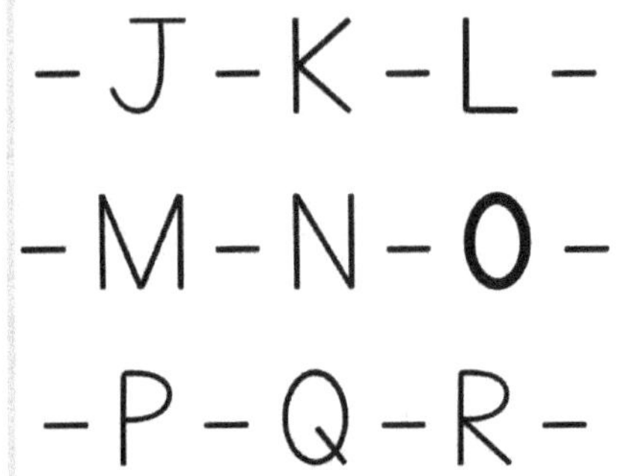

Trace

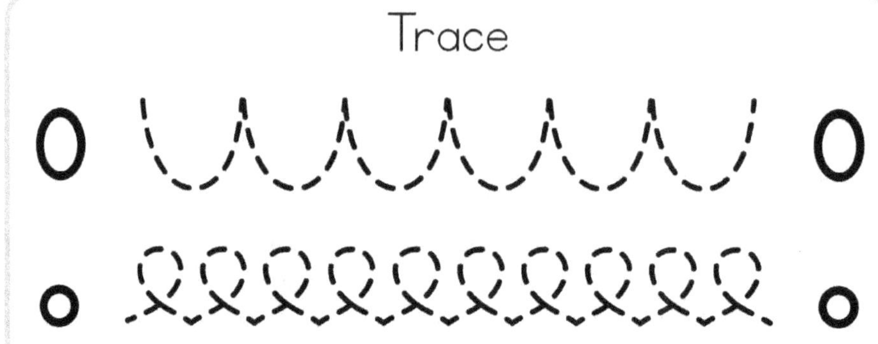

Alphabet Letters A-Z

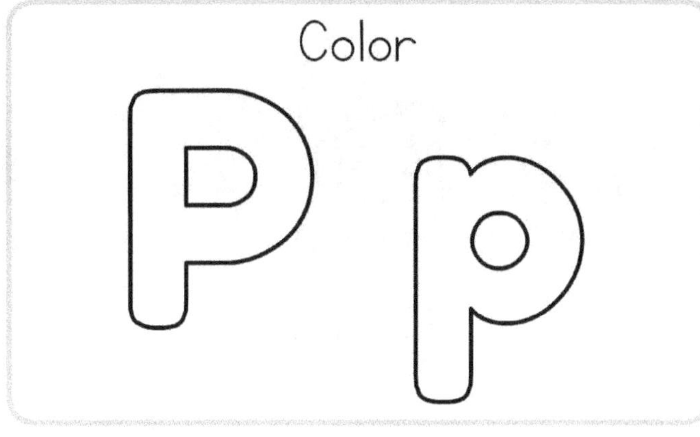

Circle it

p	P	b	p	B	b	d	P
b	B	p	P	b	P	B	p
p	P	d	p	b	p	P	d

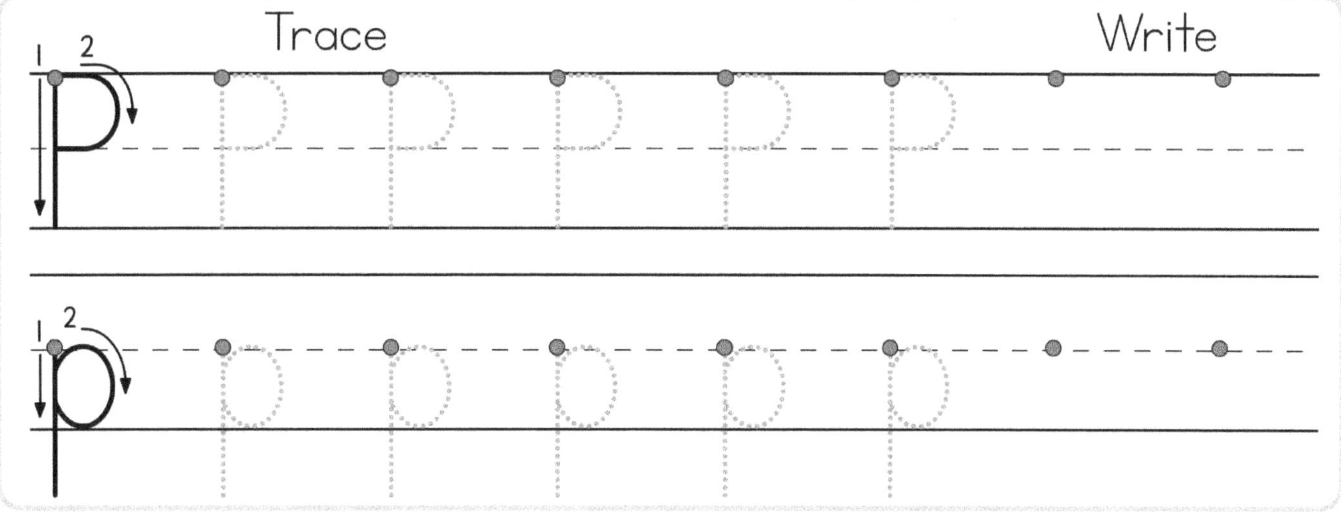

- M - N - O -
- P - Q - R -
- S - T - U -

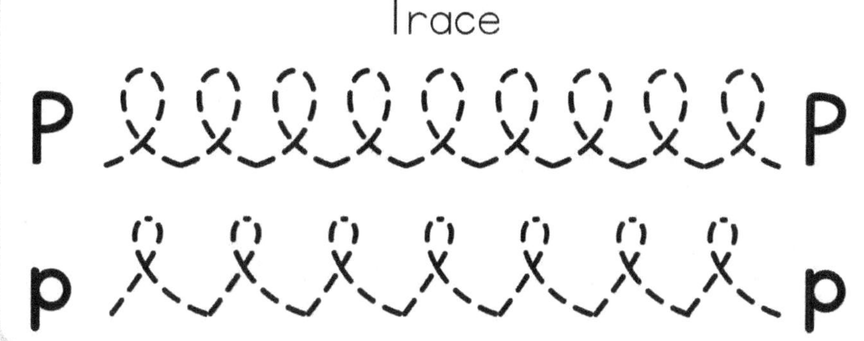

Alphabet Letters A-Z

Queen

Circle it

Q O q g q Q C q
O q Q g q C q Q
q p Q O Q g C q

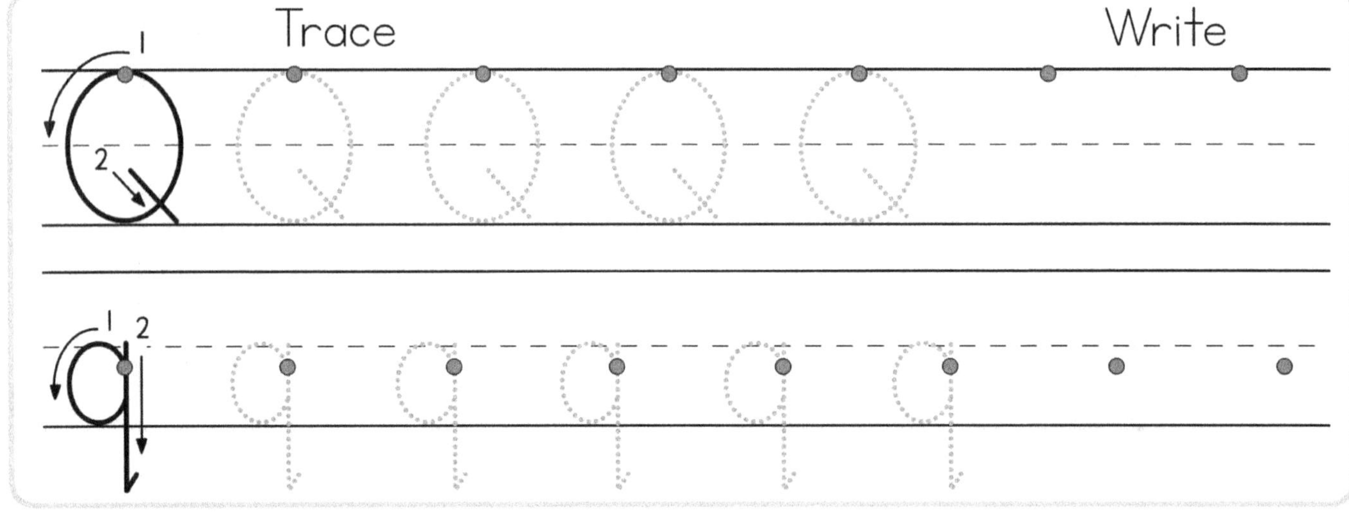

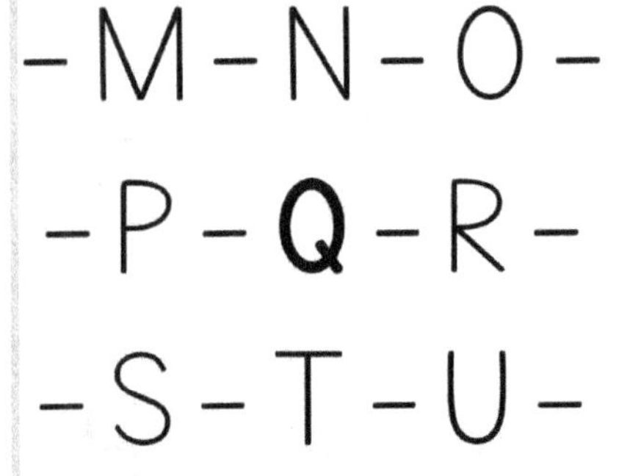

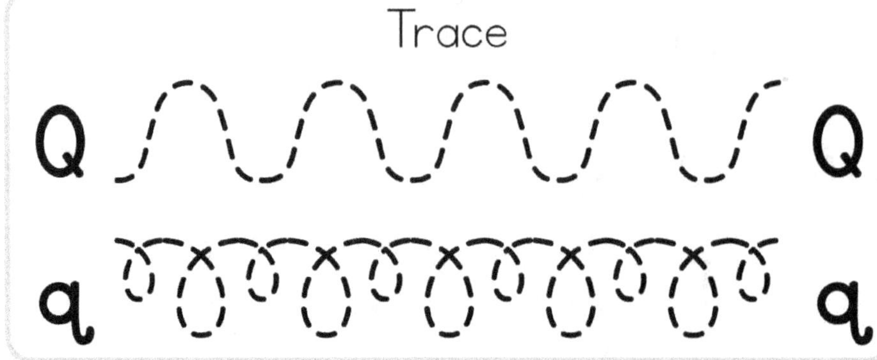

Alphabet Letters A-Z

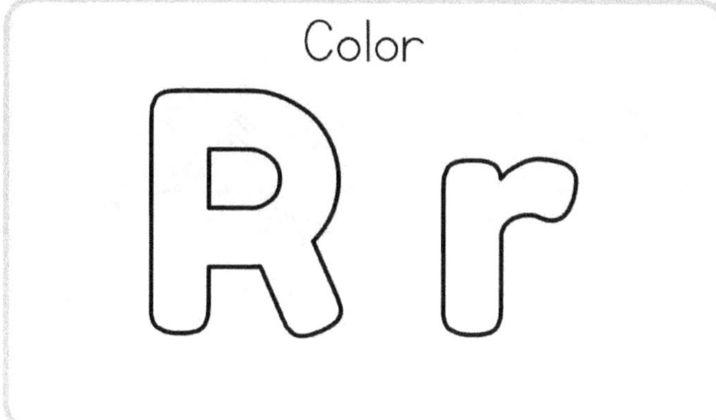

Circle it

r R r n B R P r
r r P R R n r P
n R P r n B r R

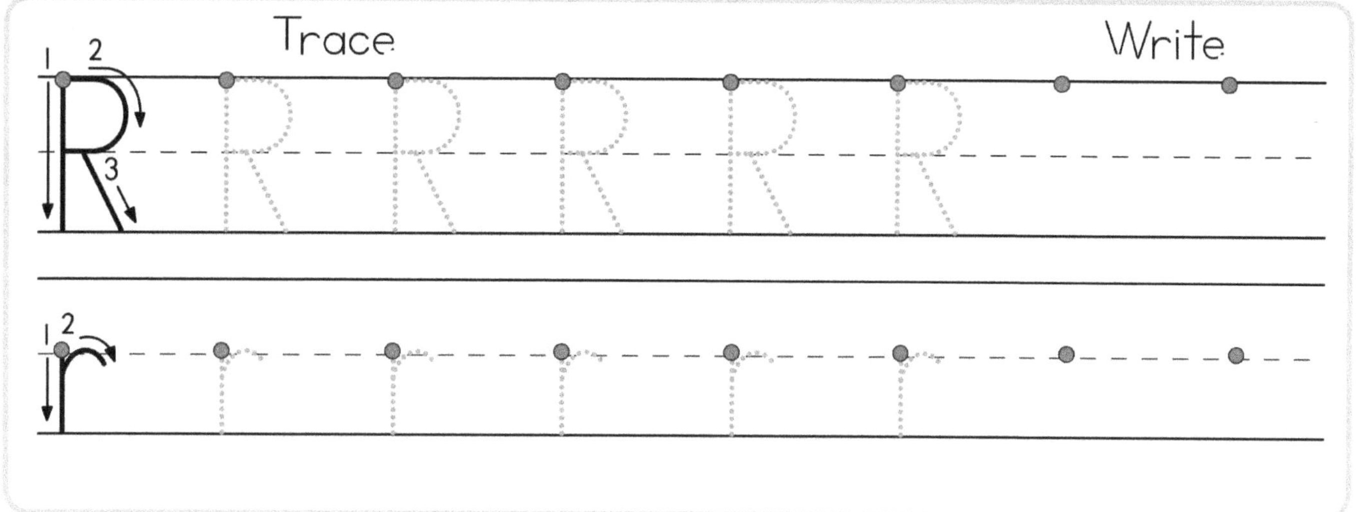

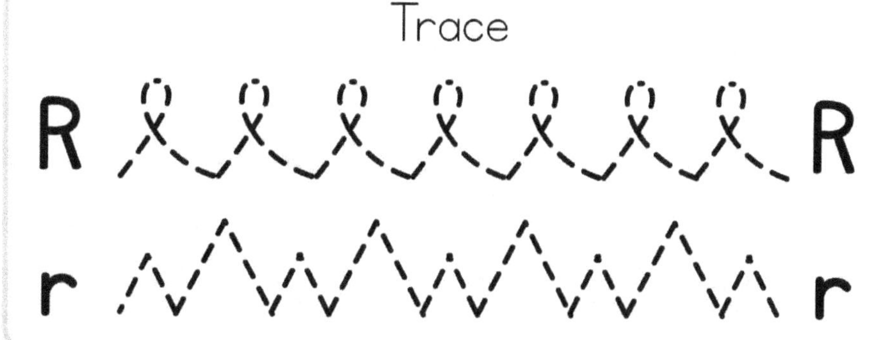

Alphabet Letters A-Z

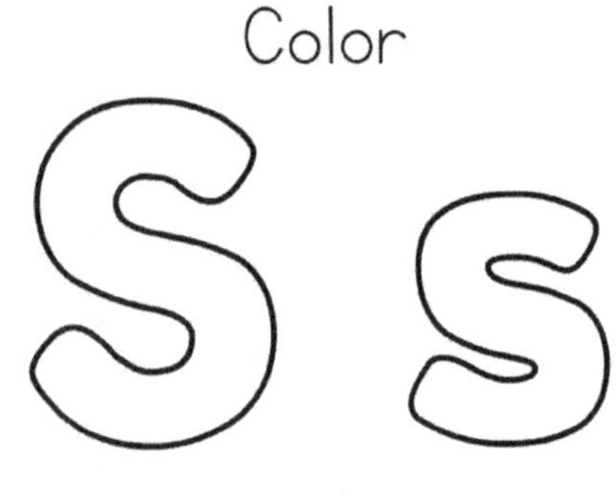

Circle it

S e s Z s S z G
Z S C e z S s z
S e s G S s C s

Snake

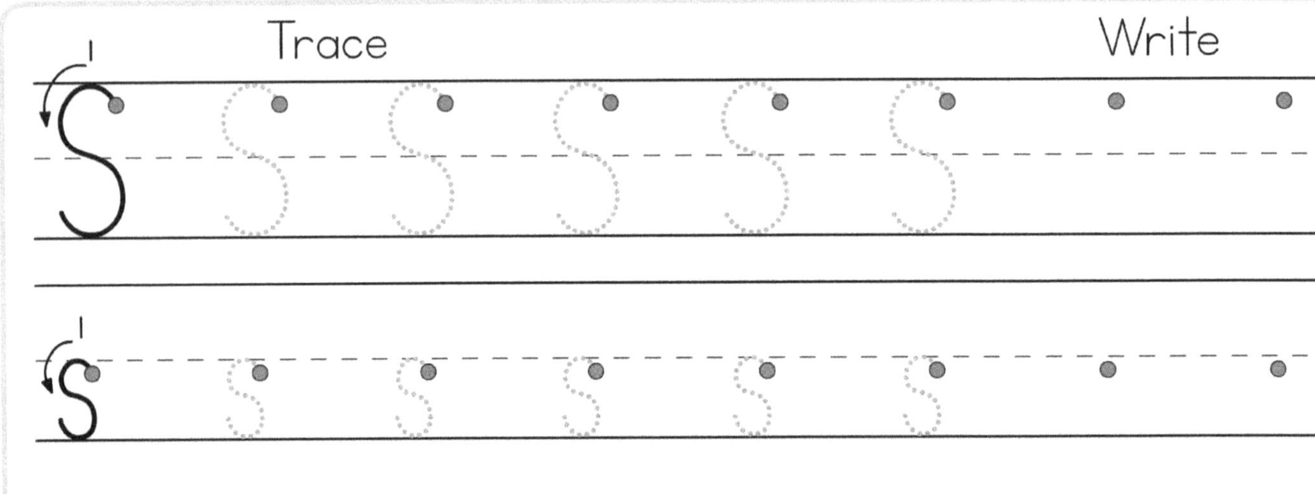

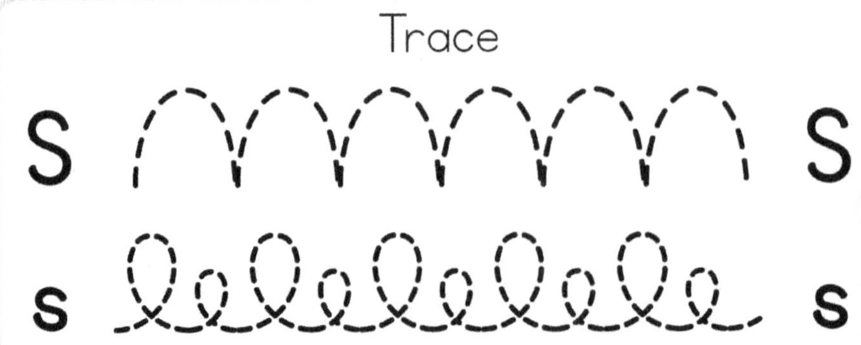

Trace

Alphabet Letters A-Z

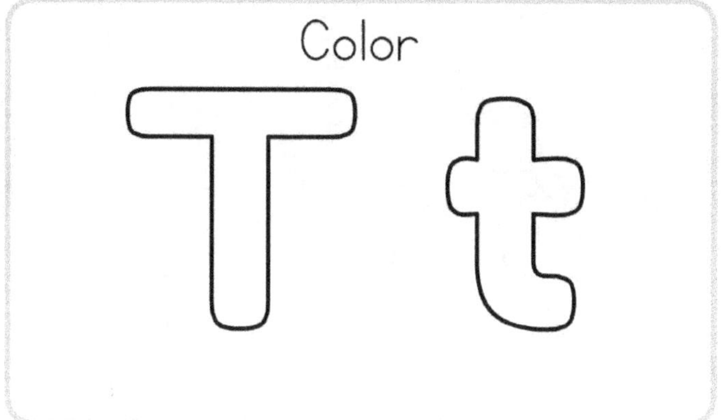

Circle it

t J I T F t f T
f t T J t L T J
T t J L I T t F

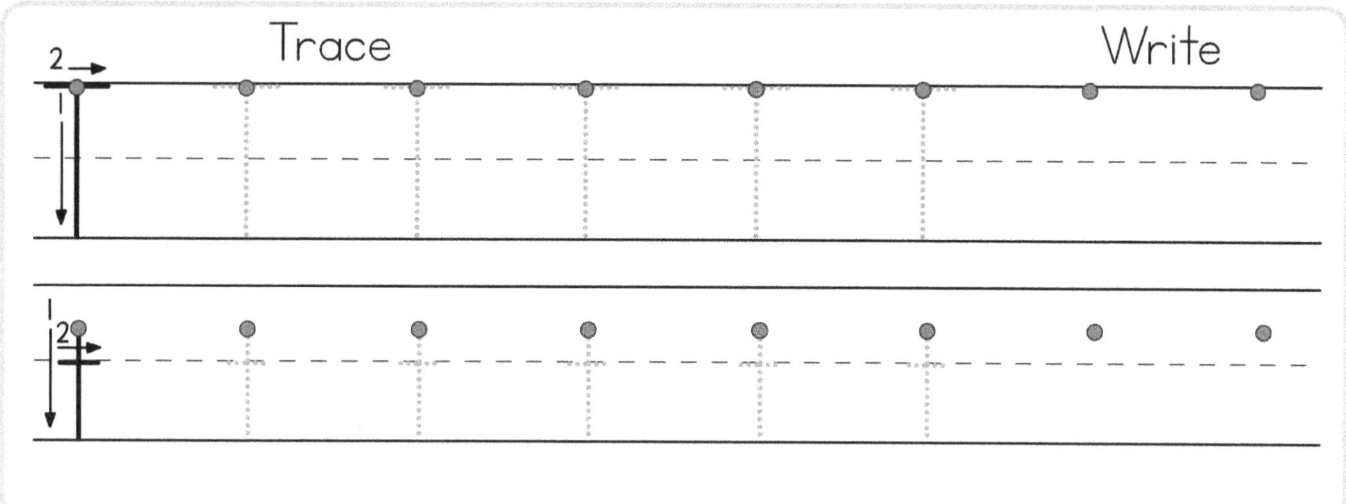

-P-Q-R-
-S-T-U-
-V-W-X-

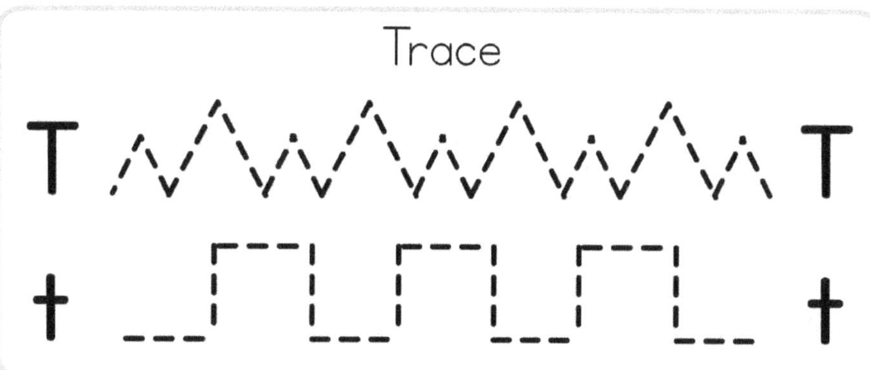

Alphabet Letters A-Z

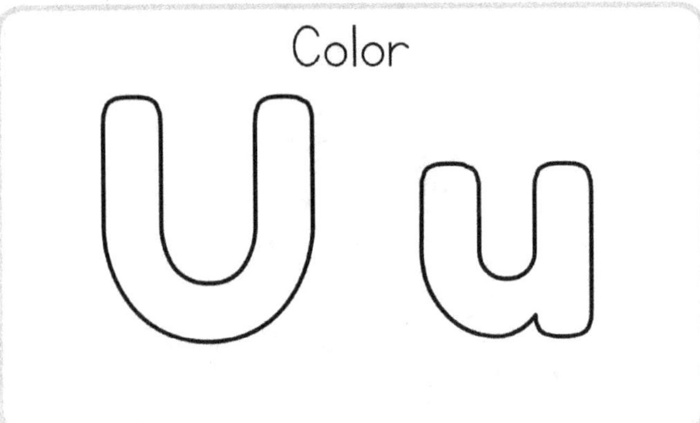

Circle it

n U V u N n U u
U u v N V u U N
u N u U v u V U

Trace   Write
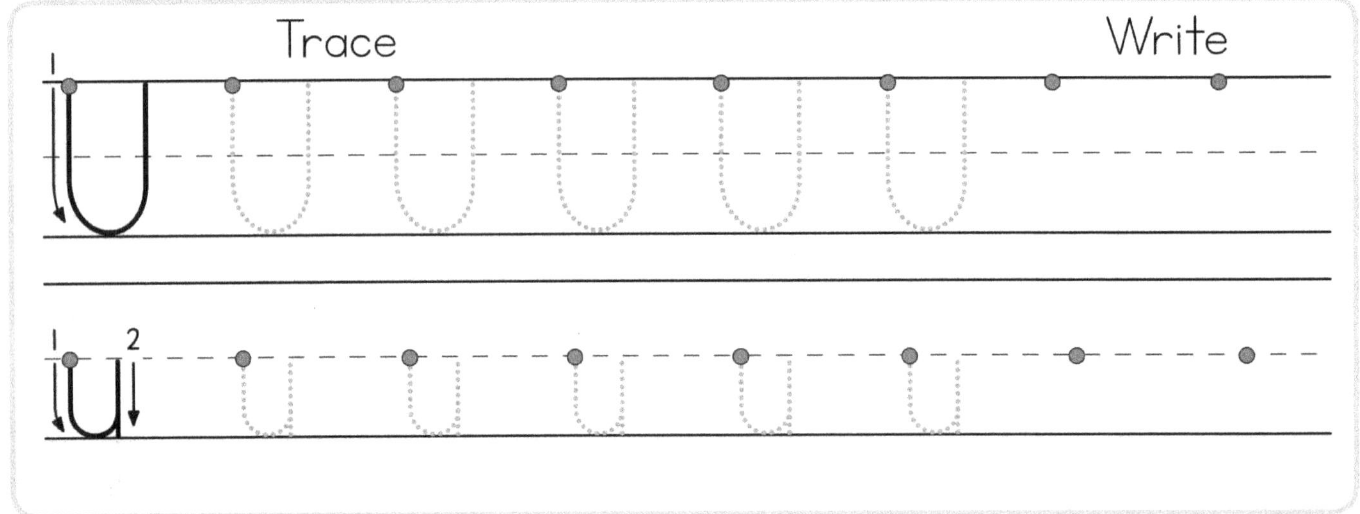

Trace
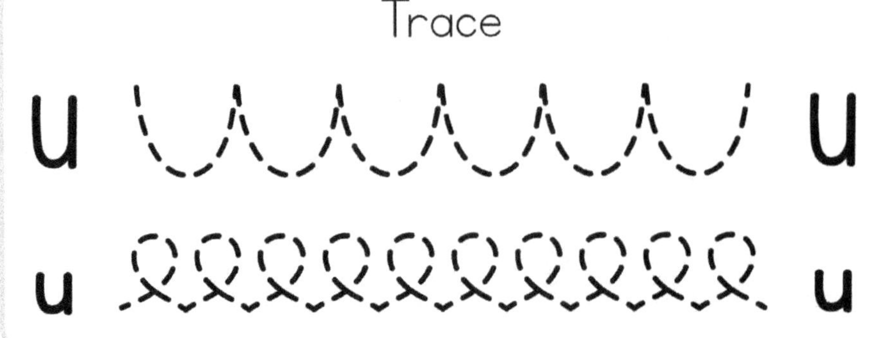

-P - Q - R -
-S - T - u -
-V - W - X -

Alphabet Letters A-Z

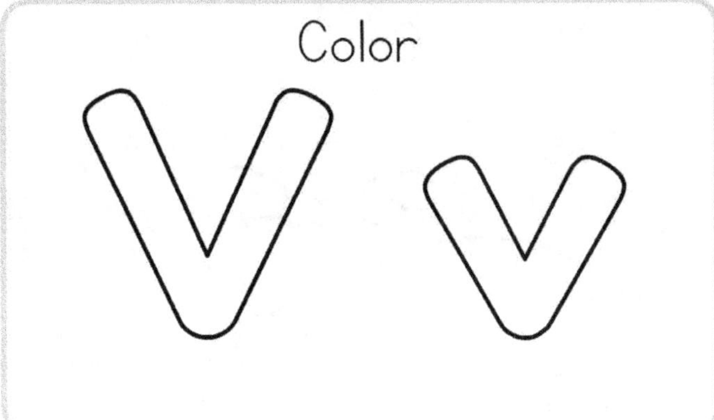

Color

Color

Volcano

Circle it

U V n v N n v V
N v u V v U V N
u V U v u V v n

Trace / Write

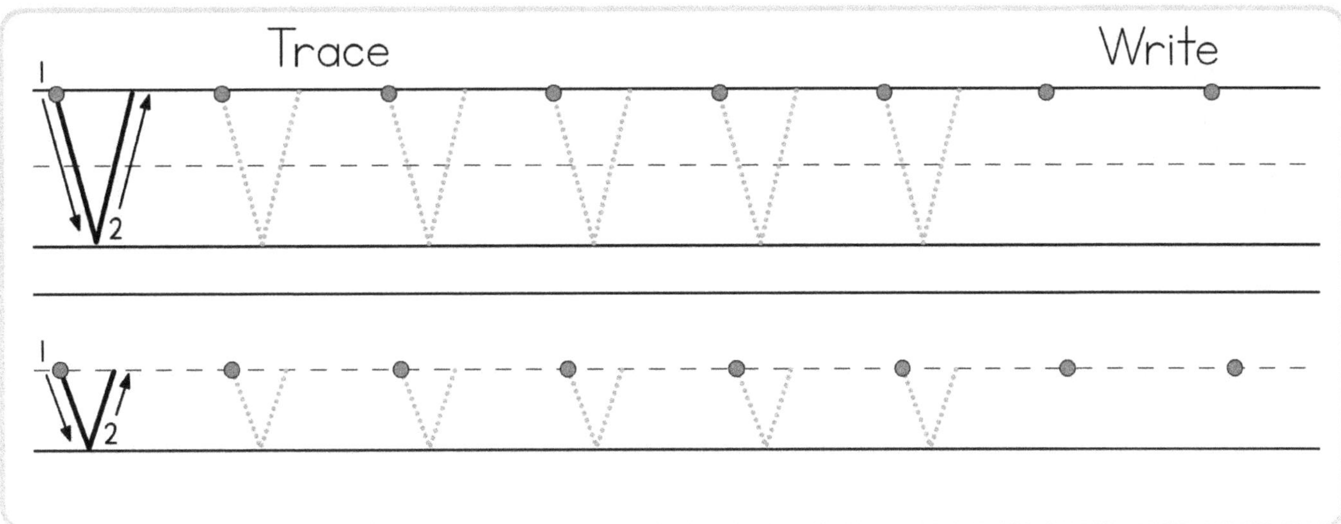

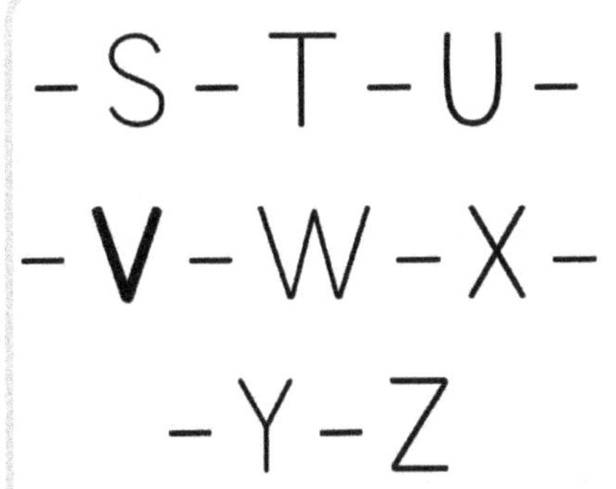

- S - T - U -
- V - W - X -
- Y - Z

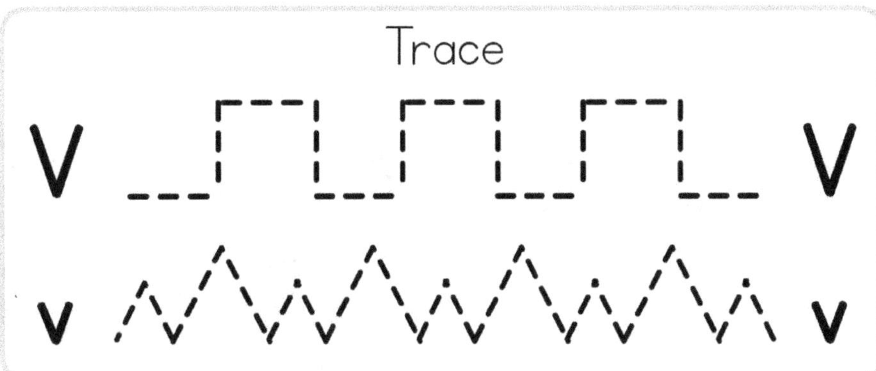

Trace

Alphabet Letters A-Z

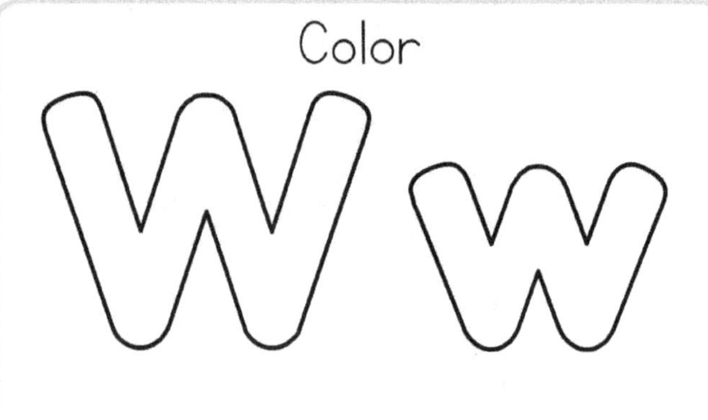

Color

Circle it

M W V w m W v
m v W M w V w
M w v m V W w

Color

Whale

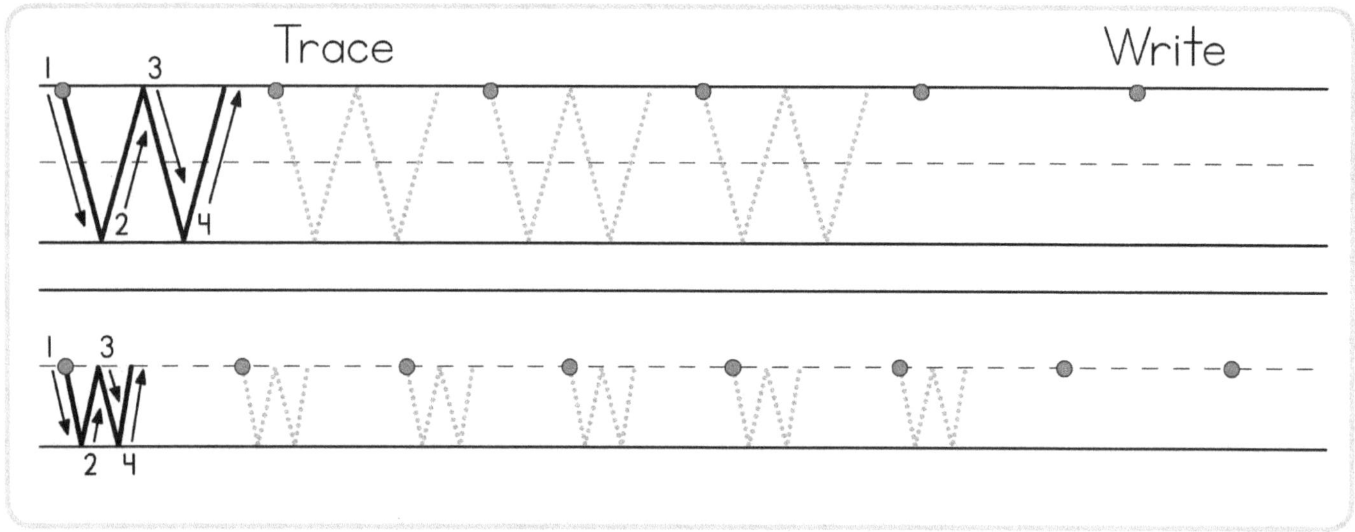

Trace

Write

- S - T - U -
- V - W - X -
- Y - Z

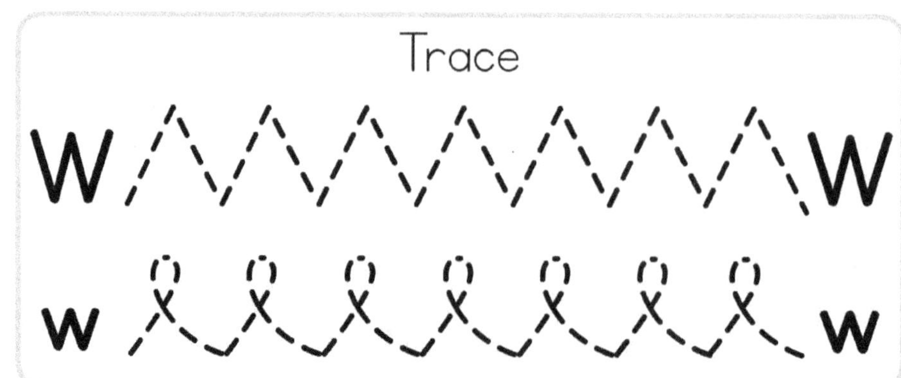

Trace

Alphabet Letters A-Z

Color

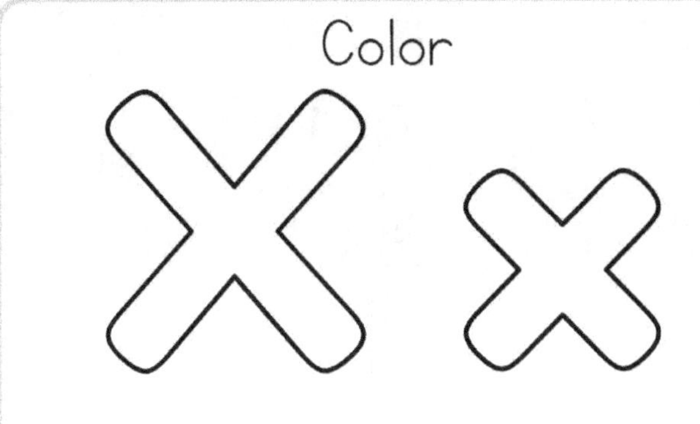

Color

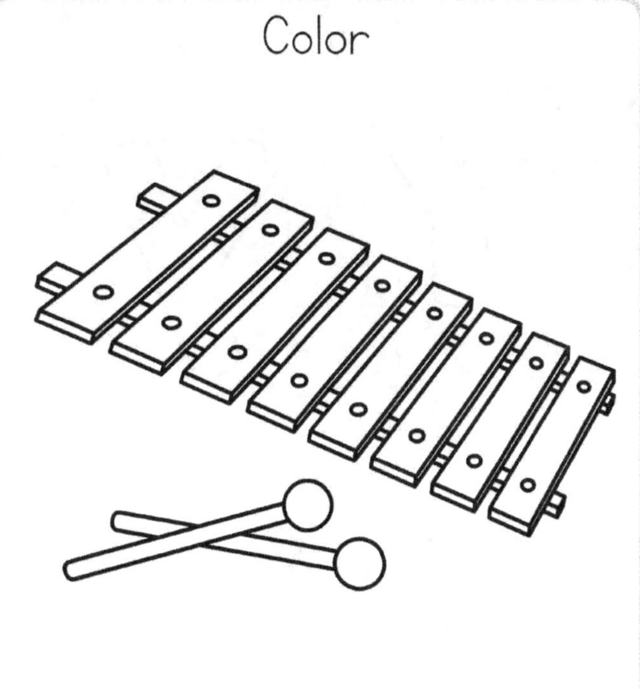

Xylophone

Circle it

V x X k K x V X
k x K V X v x X
X v x k V x K X

Trace   Write

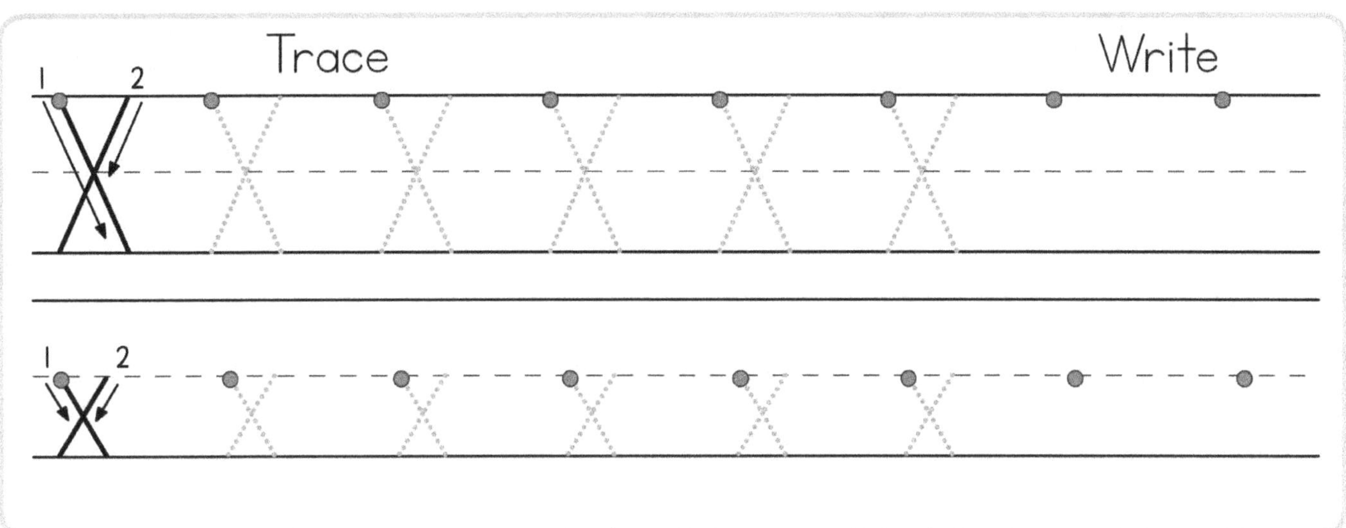

Trace

-S-T-U-
-V-W-X-
-Y-Z

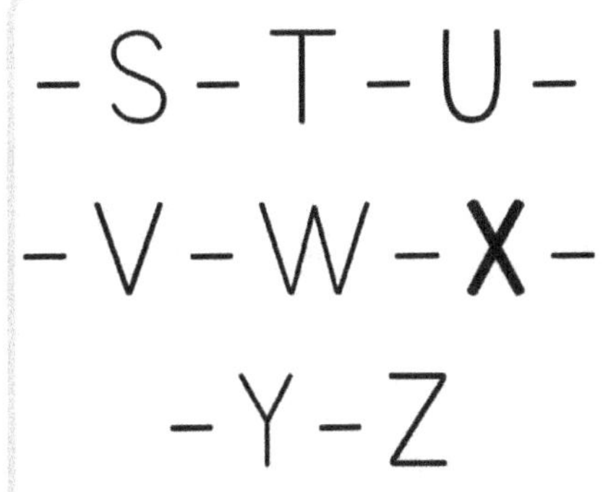

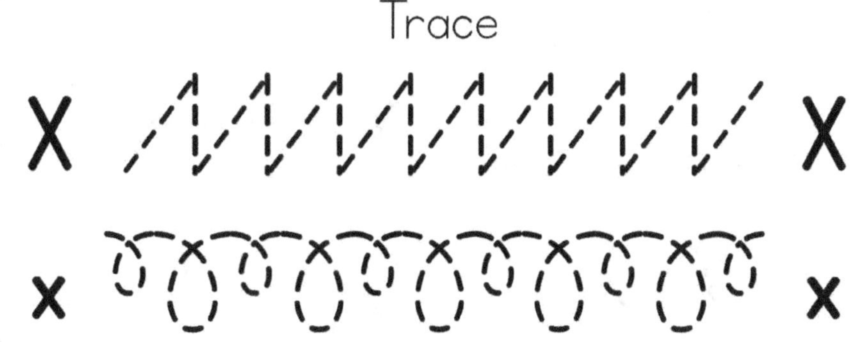

Alphabet Letters A-Z

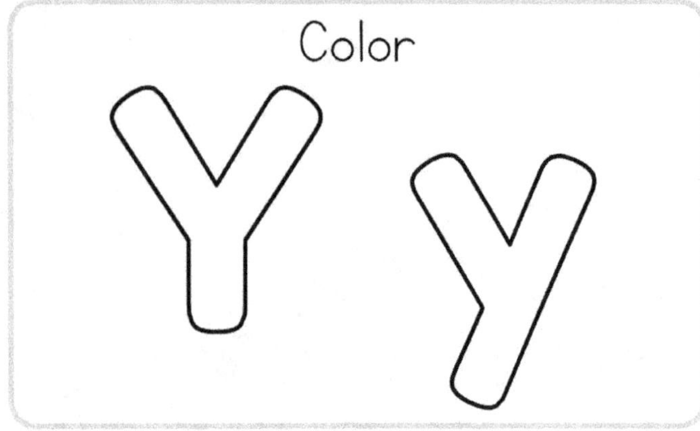

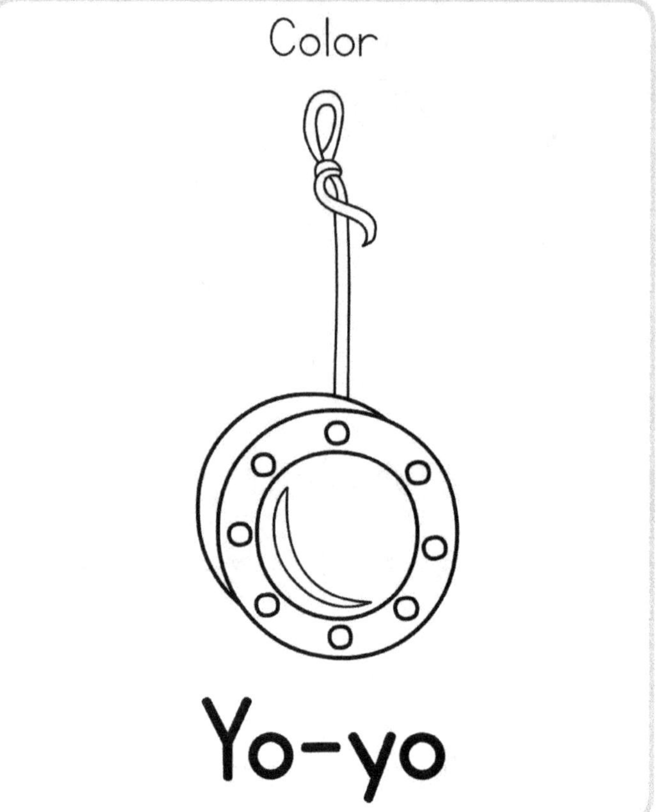

Yo-yo

Circle it

v Y U y X V Y y

y X Y u x y V Y

Y X y Y U x y V

Trace · Write

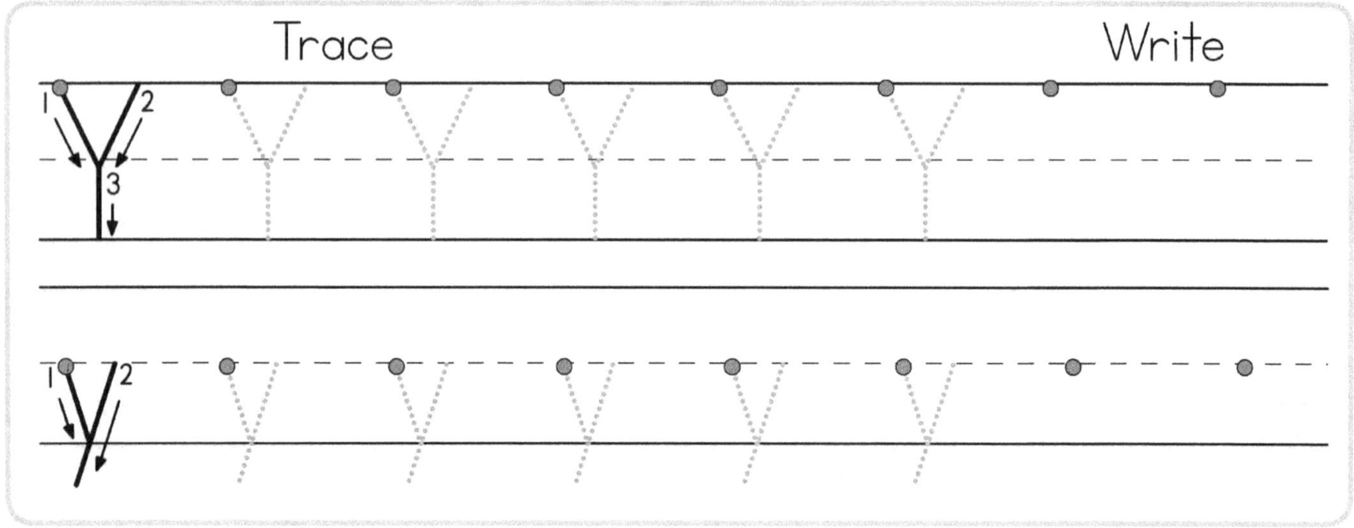

-S-T-U-

-V-W-X-

-Y-Z

Trace

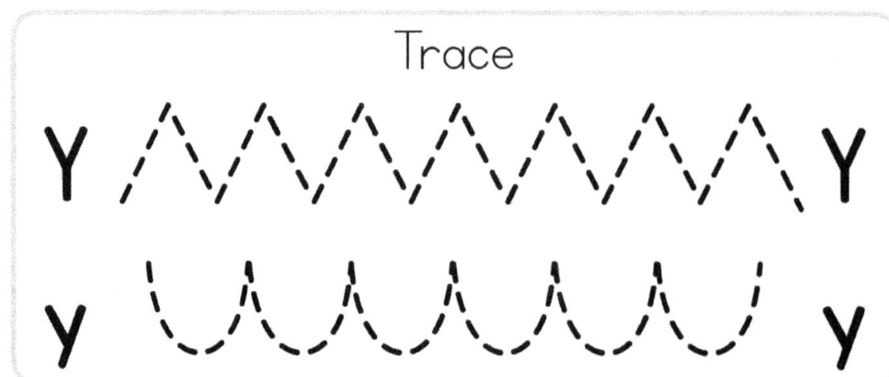

Alphabet Letters A-Z

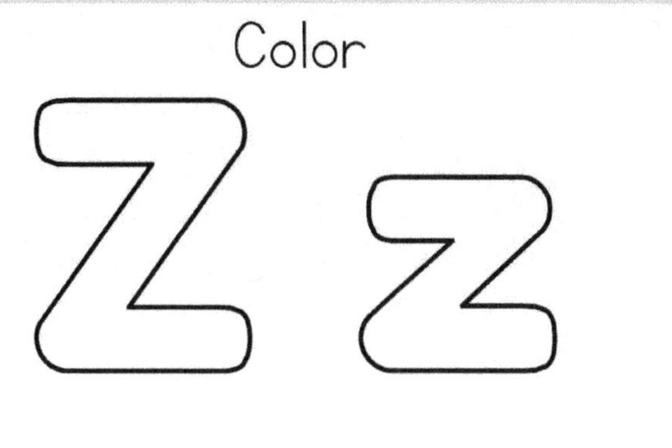

Circle it

z Z z s N Z z S
n Z S z n u Z z
Z N z S z Z u N

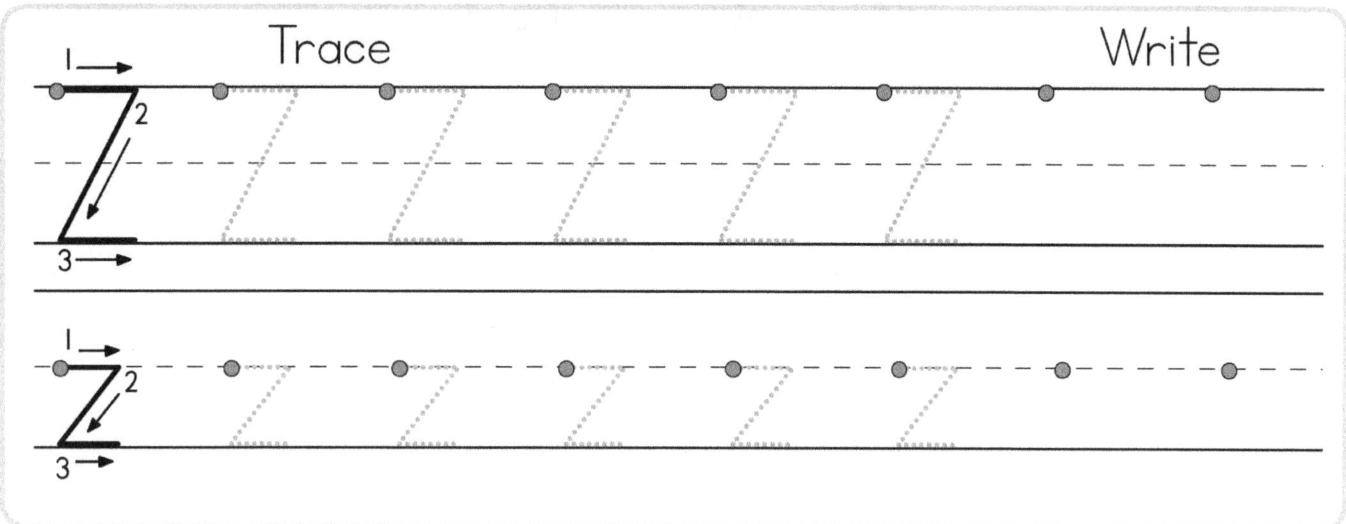

- S - T - U -
- V - W - X -
- Y - Z

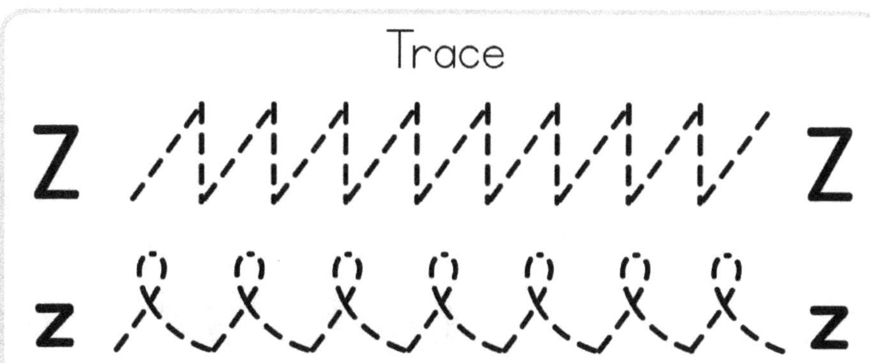

Sentence Tracing
And Cursive Letters Tracing
Tracing

Cursive A

Trace the cursive letters, then write your own.

a a a

a a a

a a a

a a a

Trace the sentence written in script.

Amanda asks

Alan about

apples.

DADAM *trace* ©

Cursive B

Trace the cursive letters, then write your own.

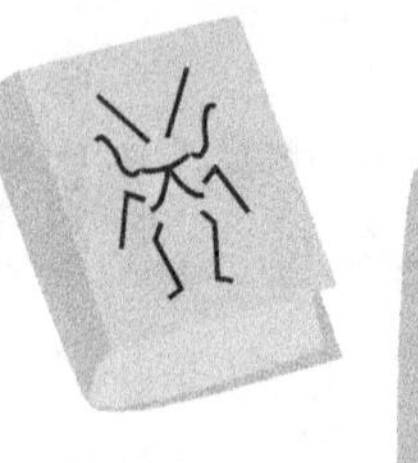
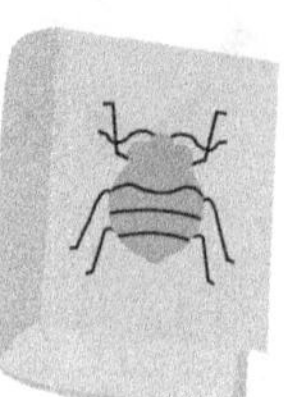

Trace the sentence written in script.

Cursive C

Trace the cursive letters, then write your own.

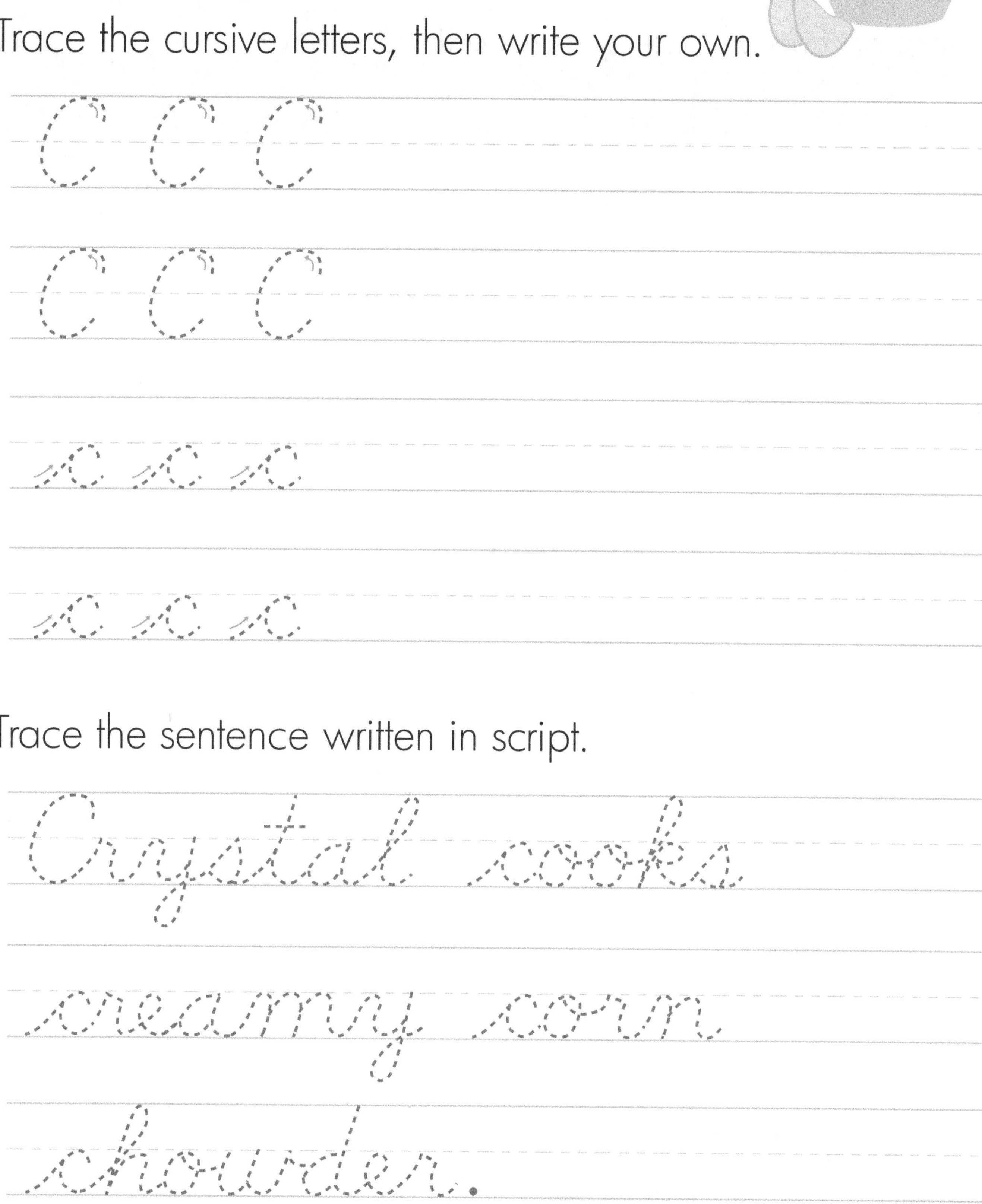

Trace the sentence written in script.

Cursive D

Trace the cursive letters, then write your own.

_D D D_

_D D D_

_d d d_

_d d d_

Trace the sentence written in script.

Cursive E

Trace the cursive letters, then write your own.

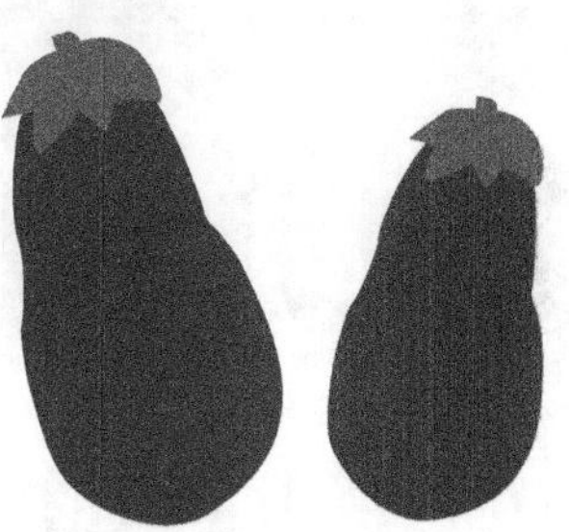

Trace the sentence written in script.

Cursive F

Trace the cursive letters, then write your own.

F F F

F F F

f f f

f f f

Trace the sentence written in script.

Fred finished first in the frog race.

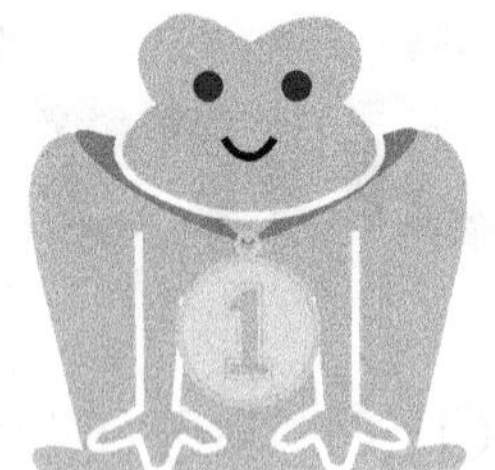

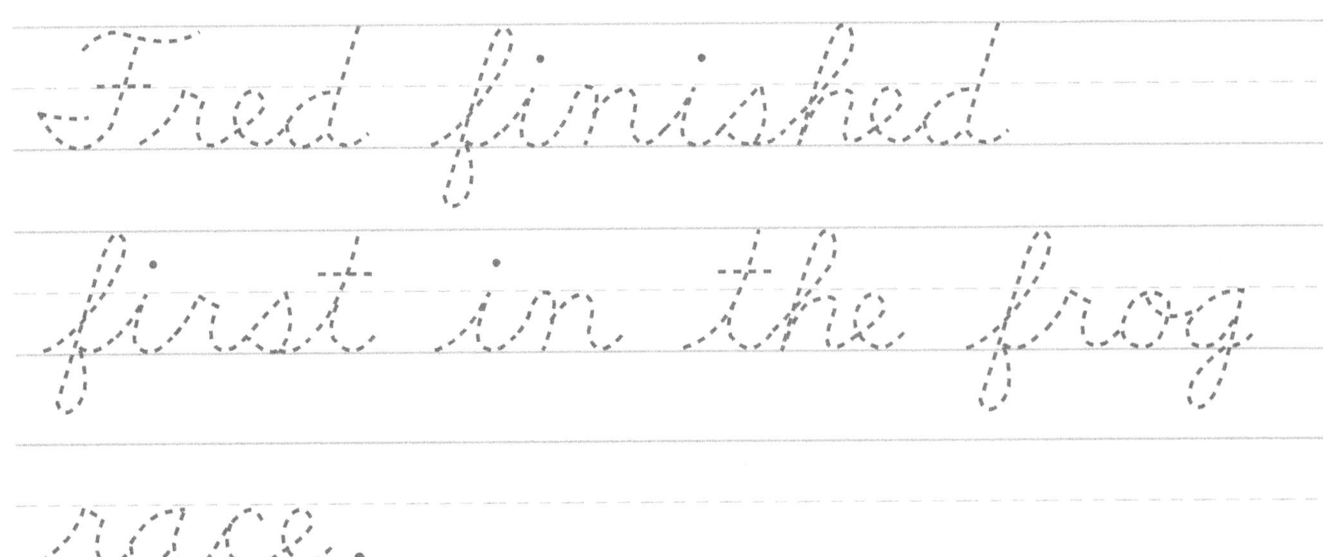

Cursive G

Trace the cursive letters, then write your own.

Trace the sentence written in script.

Cursive H

Trace the cursive letters, then write your own.

H H H

H H H

h h h

h h h

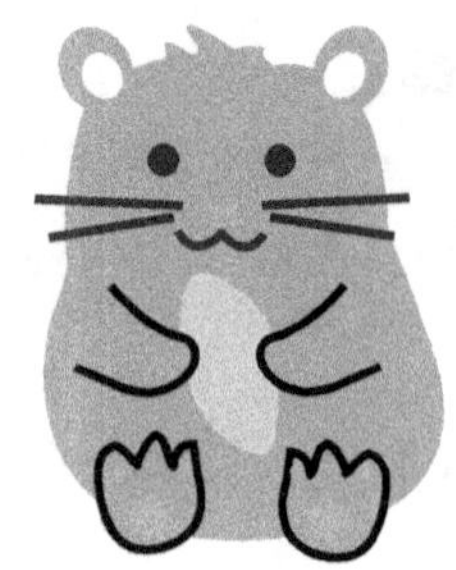

Trace the sentence written in script.

Harry has a

hairy hamster

named Herb.

Cursive I

Trace the cursive letters, then write your own.

Trace the sentence written in script.

Cursive J

Trace the cursive letters, then write your own.

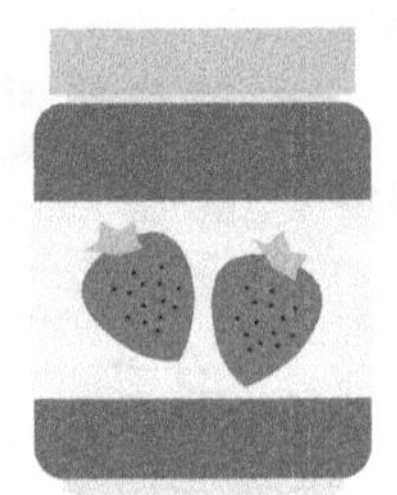

Trace the sentence written in script.

Cursive K

Trace the cursive letters, then write your own.

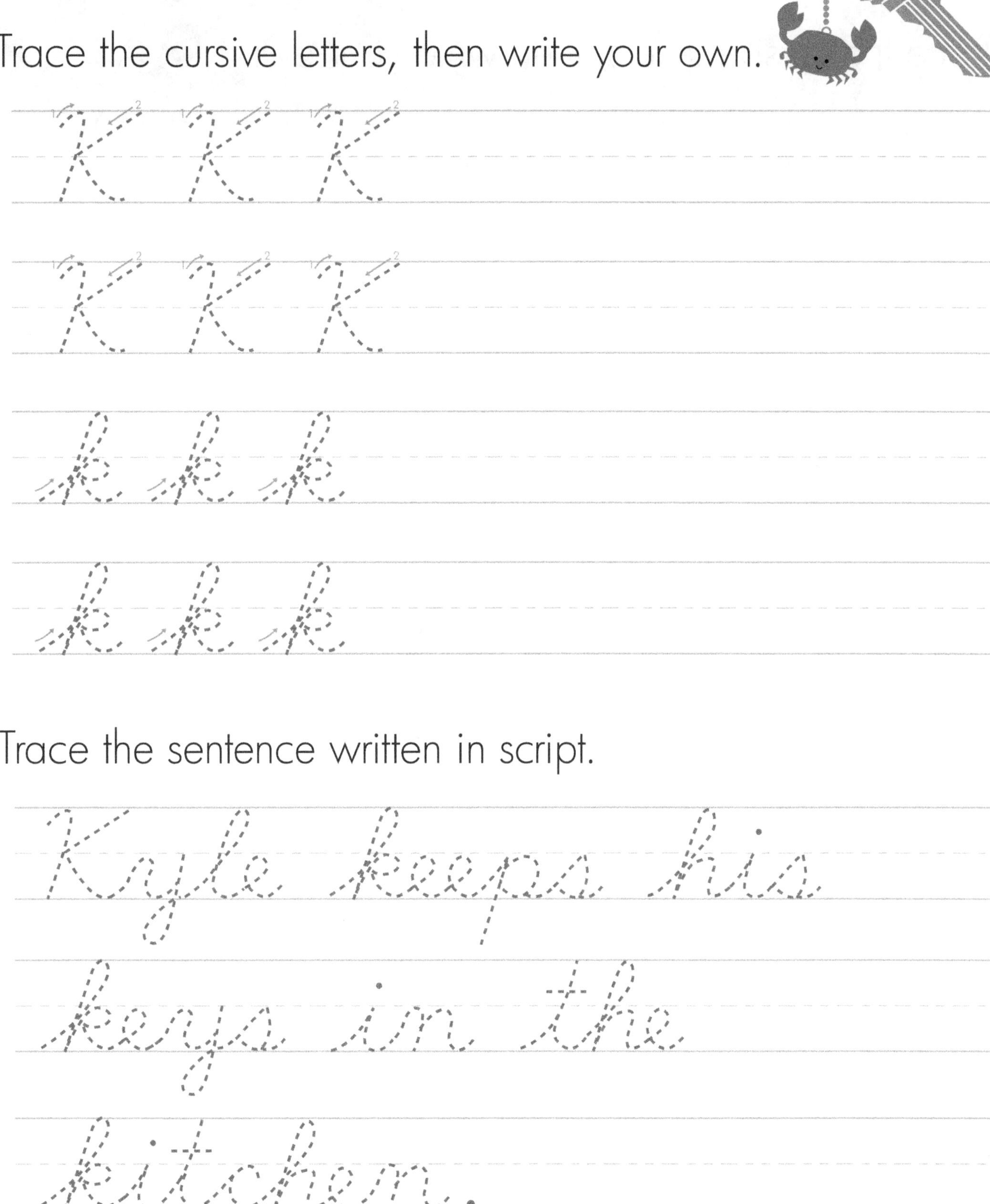

Trace the sentence written in script.

Cursive L

Trace the cursive letters, then write your own.

Trace the sentence written in script.

Cursive M

Trace the cursive letters, then write your own.

Trace the sentence written in script.

Michelle earns money making masks.

Cursive N

Trace the cursive letters, then write your own. 

Trace the sentence written in script.

Cursive O

Trace the cursive letters, then write your own.

Trace the sentence written in script.

Oliver only owns orange objects.

Cursive P

Trace the cursive letters, then write your own.

Trace the sentence written in script.

Cursive Q

Trace the cursive letters, then write your own.

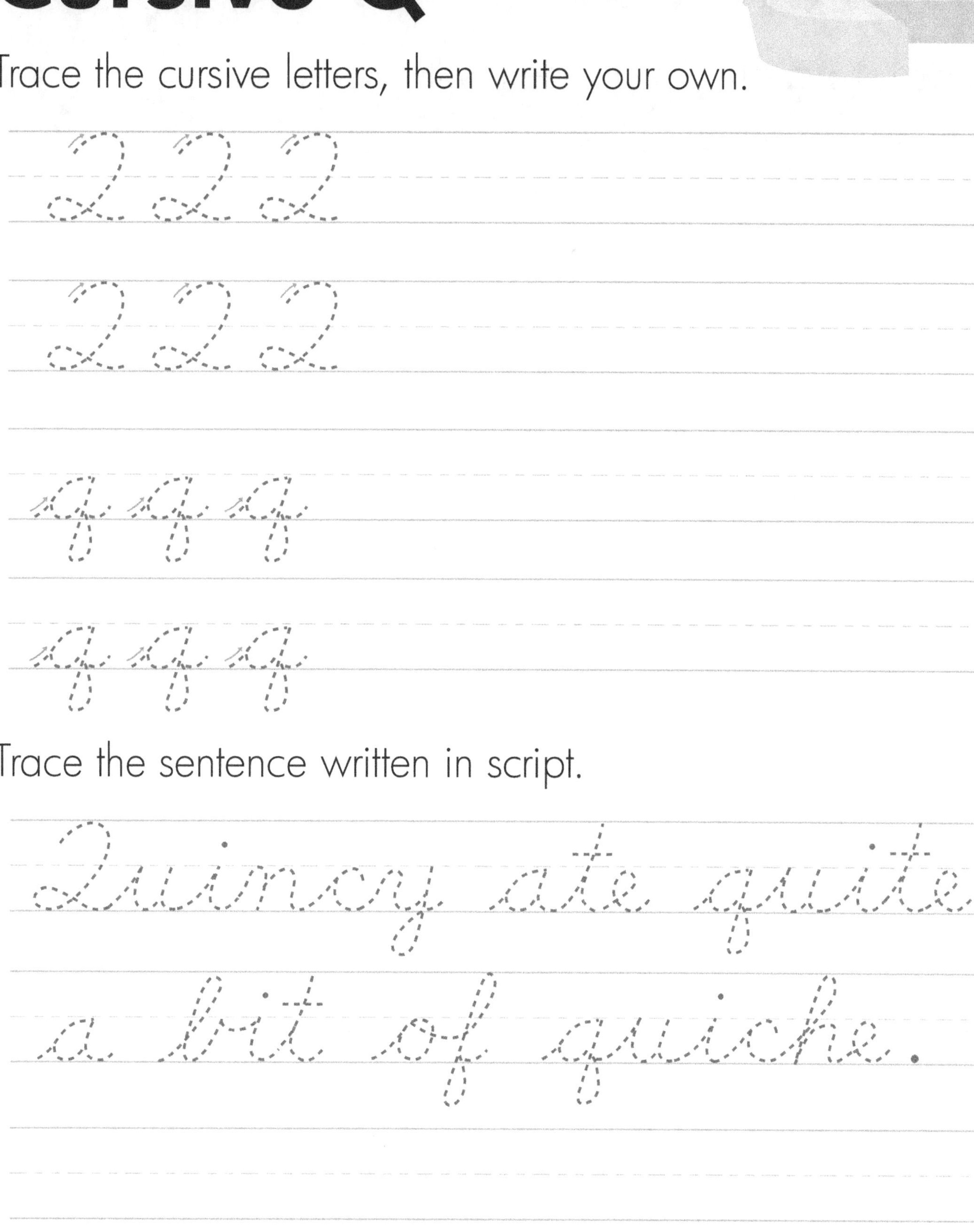

Trace the sentence written in script.

Cursive R

Trace the cursive letters, then write your own.

Trace the sentence written in script.

Cursive S

Trace the cursive letters, then write your own.

Trace the sentence written in script.

Samantha sails on the sea every Saturday.

Cursive T

Trace the cursive letters, then write your own.

Trace the sentence written in script.

Cursive U

Trace the cursive letters, then write your own.

Trace the sentence written in script.

Cursive V

Trace the cursive letters, then write your own.

Trace the sentence written in script.

Cursive W

Trace the cursive letters, then write your own.

Trace the sentence written in script.

Will wishes

winter were

warmer.

Cursive X

Trace the cursive letters, then write your own.

Trace the sentence written in script.

Xander took some excellent X-rays.

Cursive Y

Trace the cursive letters, then write your own.

Trace the sentence written in script.

Cursive Z

Trace the cursive letters, then write your own.

Trace the sentence written in script.

Trace letters
and exercises

DADAM *trace* ©

Name ____________________

Aa is for .

DADAM *trace* ©

Page Instructions: Help the student read, "A is for apple." Say, "Repeat the names of the pictures after me: apples, alligator, astronaut. What sound do you hear at the beginning of each word?" Tell the student to trace the letters in the boxes, start at the big dot. Color the page.

Activity: Play this game. Say, "I am going to say a word. Clap your hands if the word you hear starts with the /a/ sound. "
Word List: apple, alligator, ax, pig, tree, astronaut, adventure, fish, alphabet, dog.

Aa

Page Instructions: Make your own "Aa" page. Draw, cut and paste pictures that start with the /a/ sound. Cut and paste words with the letter A from magazines or newspapers. Use the lines to practice writing letters and/or copy simple words & sentences.

Activity: Make three boxes on the board. Write the short vowel in the middle box. Add beginning and ending consonants such as "c" and "t." Track as you segment and blend the word: /c/-/a/-/t/, /cat/. Say, "Let's think of more words that have /a/ in the middle, like CAT." Give additional clues if students are having difficulty.

Word List: back, bag, basket, bath, black, cab, can, cat, class, crack, dad, fan, fast, flag, glass, grass, ham, jack, lamp, lap, last, man, map, mask, mat, math, nap, pants, plant, ran, rat, sad, sand, snap, splash, tag, tan, van.

Name ____

Page Instructions: Tell the student to point to the capital-A basket. Say "Color the capital-A on the basket RED. Color the apples in the basket RED too." Tell the student to point to the lower-case-a basket. Say "Color the lower-case-a on the basket YELLOW. Color the apples in the basket YELLOW too." "Now we are going to color the apples in the tree. Color all the capital-A apples RED, and all the lower-case-a apples YELLOW, just like the ones in the baskets."

Name ______________________________

Aa

Aa

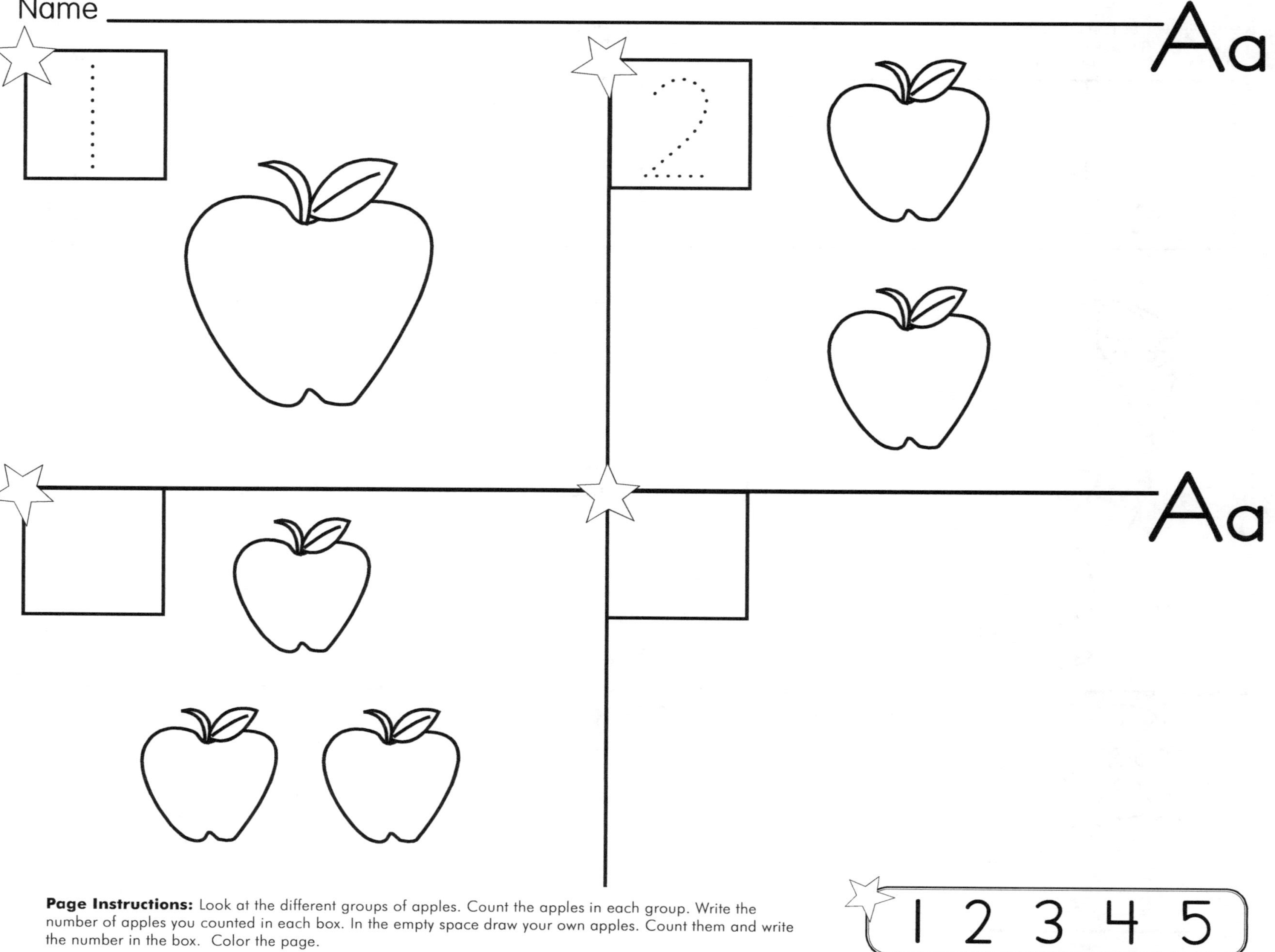

Page Instructions: Look at the different groups of apples. Count the apples in each group. Write the number of apples you counted in each box. In the empty space draw your own apples. Count them and write the number in the box. Color the page.

1 2 3 4 5

Name ___________________________

Bb is for 

Page Instructions: Help the student read, "B is for bike." Say, "Repeat the names of the pictures after me: ball, boy, bear. What sound do you hear at the beginning of each word?" Tell the student to trace the letters in the boxes, start at the big dot. Color the page.

Activity: Play this game. Say, "I am going to say a word, listen carefully to it. If it starts with the /b/ sound, give me thumbs up! If it doesn't start with the /b/ sound, give me thumbs down."

Word List: baby, big, blue, bell, boy, table, bike, desk, book, cat, bird, fish, bed, hat, banana.

B b

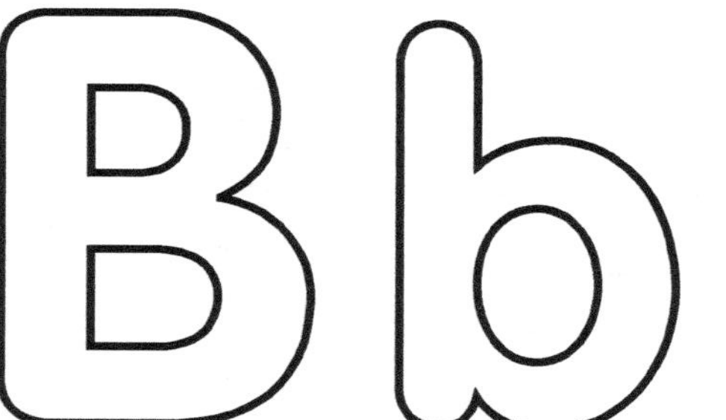

Page Instructions: Make your own "Bb" page. Draw or cut and paste pictures that start with the /b/ sound onto the page. Use the writing lines to practice letter shapes or copy simple sentences.

Activity: Play this game. Say, "Let's go around the room and everyone say a word that starts with the /b/ sound." Give additional clues if students are having difficulty.
Word List: baby, bag, ball, balloons, banana, barn, baseball, bat, beach, bear, bed, bell, between, big, before, bike, black, blocks, blue, bone, book, boots, box, bread, bridge, brown, bubbles, bus, buttons, boat, birthday.

Name ______________________________

Cc

C C   is for   .

Page Instructions: Help the student read, "C is for cat." Say, "Repeat the names of the pictures after me: cow, computer, cookies. What sound do you hear at the beginning of each word?" Tell the student to trace the letters in the boxes, start at the big dot. Color the page.

Activity: Play this game. Say, "I am going to say a word, listen carefully to it. If it starts with the /k/ sound, stand up! If it doesn't start with the /k/ sound, sit down."

Word List: cat, clean, corn, dig, cake, water, candy, fan, cow, barn, cookies, carrot, lips, color.

Page Instructions: Make your own "Cc" page. Draw or cut and paste pictures that start with the /k/ sound onto the page. Use the writing lines to practice letter shapes or copy simple sentences.

Activity: Play this game. Say, "Let's go around the room and everyone say a word that starts with the /k/ sound." Give additional clues if students are having difficulty.

Word List: cabin, cake, calculator, camera, can, candy, candle, car, carrots, cat, catch, caterpillar, cave, click, clock, clown, colors, cook, cool, cold, corn, cow, crayon, cry, cup, castle, count.

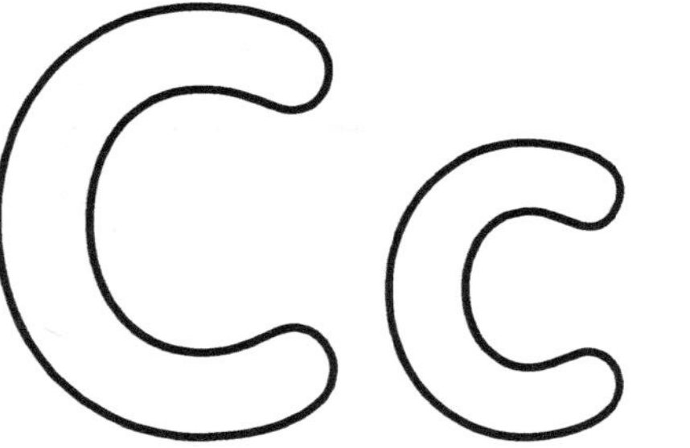

Name ___________________________________

Dd is for _______ .

Page Instructions: Help the student read, "D is for doll." Say, "Repeat the names of the pictures after me: drum, duck, dinosaurs. What sound do you hear at the beginning of each word?" Tell the student to trace the letters in the boxes, start at the big dot. Color the page.

Activity: Play this game. Line up students at the back of the room. Say, "I am going to say a word. Take one step forward if the word you hear starts with the /d/ sound."
Word List: duck, dig, apple, dog, day, fish, different, down, cow, door, desk, car, dot.

Dd

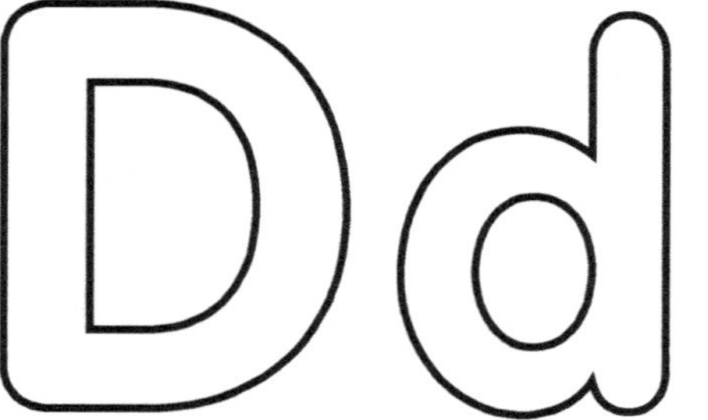

Page Instructions: Make your own "Dd" page. Draw or cut and paste pictures that start with the /d/ sound onto the page. Use the writing lines to practice letter shapes or copy simple sentences.

Activity: Play this game. Say, "Let's go around the room and everyone say a word that starts with the /d/ sound." Give additional clues if students are having difficulty.

Word List: dad, dalmatian, danger, deep, deer, desk, dice, different, dig, dinosaur, dirty, diver, doctor, dog, doll, dolphin, donuts, door, dot, down, dragon, dragonfly, draw, dream, dress, drip, drive, drum, duck, day.

Name ___________________________

Ee is for

Page Instructions: Help the student read, "E is for eggs." Say, "Repeat the names of the pictures after me: enter, elephant, exit. What sound do you hear at the beginning of each word?" Tell the student to trace the letters in the boxes, start at the big dot. Color the page.

Activity: Play this game. Be sure each student has a YES and NO card. Say, "I am going to say a word. If you think the word starts with the /e/ sound, hold up your YES card. If you think the word does NOT start with the /e/ sound, hold up your NO card."

Word List: elbow, exercise, eggs, rain, enter, paint, exit, moon, elevator, empty, excellent!

Page Instructions: Make your own "Ee" page. Draw, cut and paste pictures that start with the /e/ sound. Cut and paste words with the letter E from magazines or newspapers. Use the lines to practice writing letters and/or copy simple words & sentences.

Activity: Make three boxes on the board. Write the short vowel in the middle box. Add beginning and ending consonants such as "b" and "d." Track as you segment and blend the word: /b/-/e/-/d/, /bed/. Say, "Let's think of more words that have /e/ in the middle, like BED." Give additional clues if students are having difficulty.

Word List: bell, belt, bench, best, desk, dress, fell, fresh, get, help, hen, jet, left, leg, less, let, men, mess, neck, net, pen, pet, red, rest, sell, send, set, shell, sled, smell, spell, step, tell, ten, tent, test, vest, vet, web, well, wet, yell, yes.

Name

Page Instructions: Tell the student to point to the capital-E nest. Say "Color the capital-E on the nest BLUE. Color the eggs in the nest BLUE too." Tell the student to point to the lower-case-e nest. Say "Color the lower-case-e on the nest YELLOW. Color the eggs in the nest YELLOW too." "Now we are going to help sort out the eggs on the farm. Color all the capital-E eggs BLUE, and all the lower-case-e eggs YELLOW, just like the ones in the nests."

Name _______________________

Ee

Ee

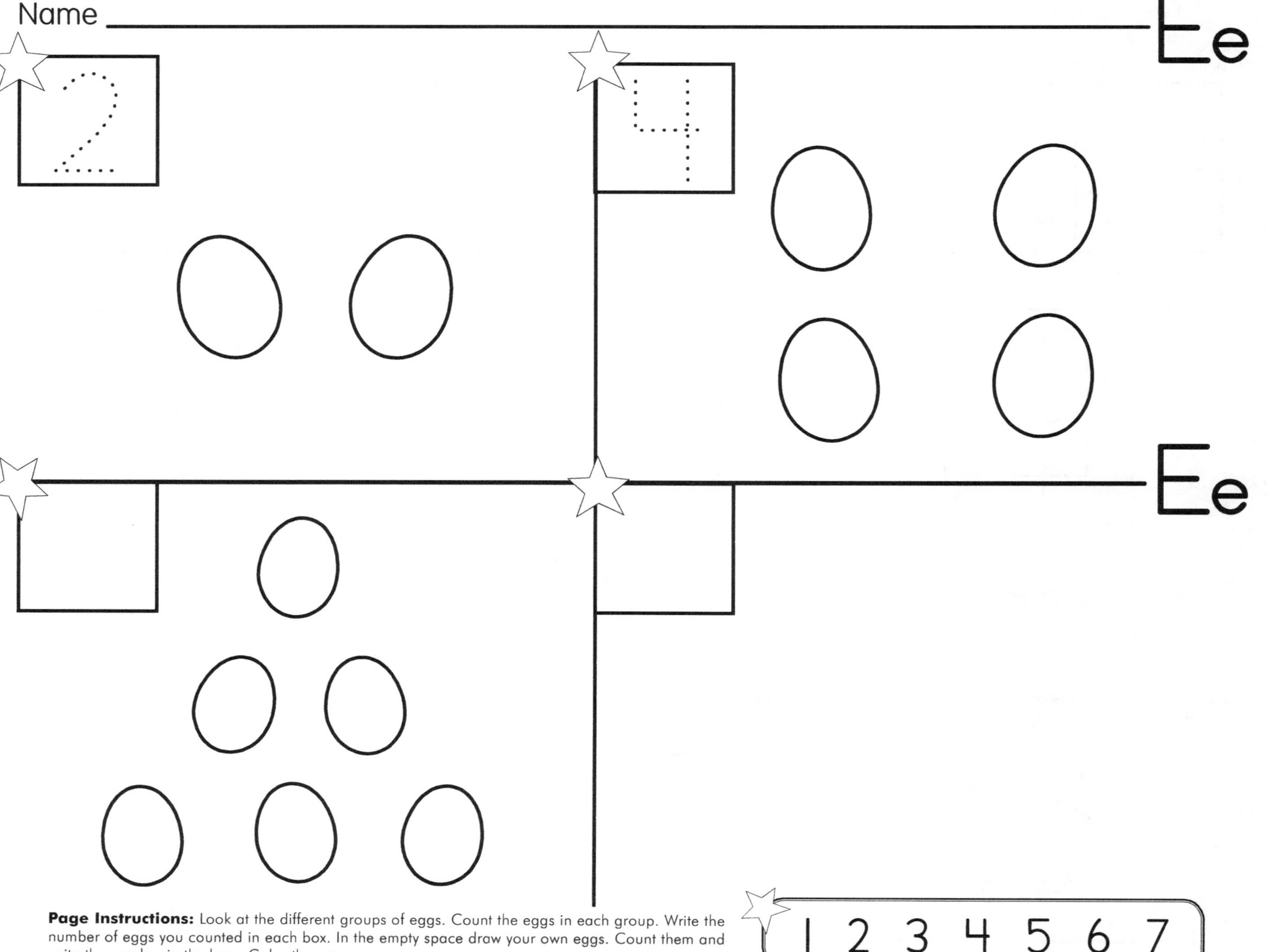

Page Instructions: Look at the different groups of eggs. Count the eggs in each group. Write the number of eggs you counted in each box. In the empty space draw your own eggs. Count them and write the number in the box. Color the page.

1 2 3 4 5 6 7

Name ____________________

Ff is for 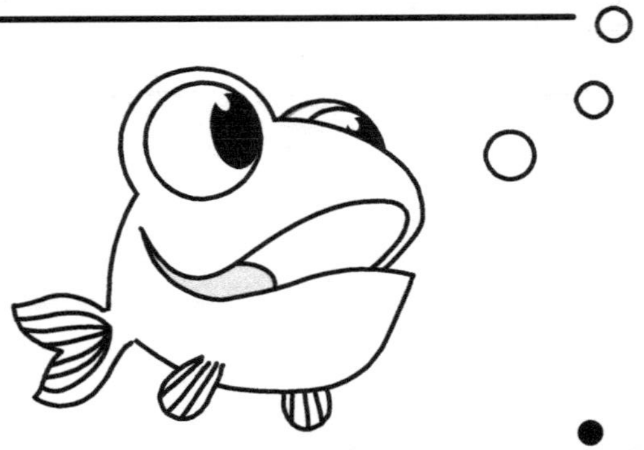.

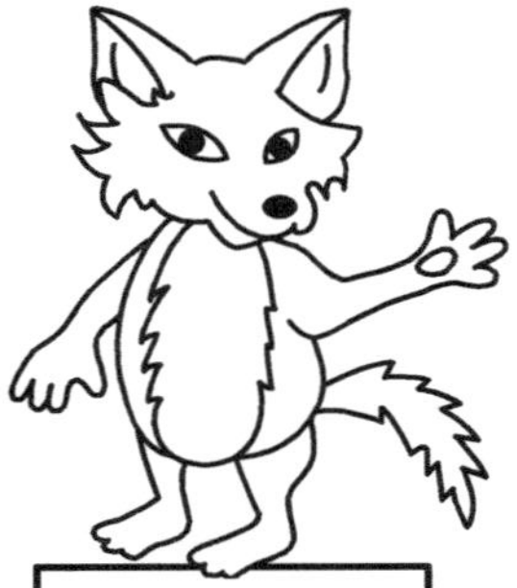

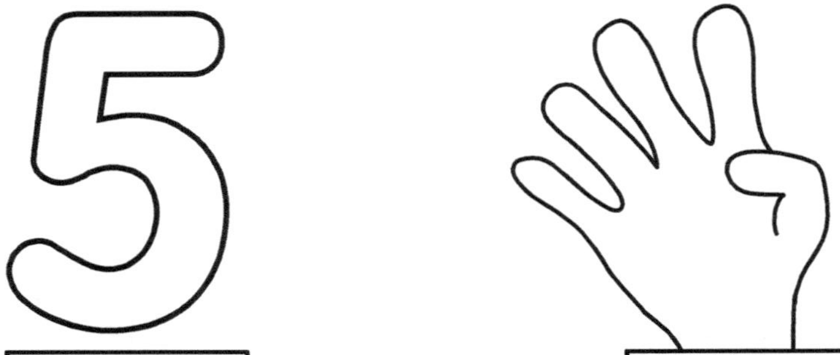

Page Instructions: Help the student read, "F is for fish." Say, "Repeat the names of the pictures after me: fox, five, four fingers. What sound do you hear at the beginning of each word?" Tell the student to trace the letters in the boxes, start at the big dot. Color the page.

Activity: Play this game. Say, "I am going to say a word. Put your hands on your head if the word you hear starts with the /f/ sound. Keep your hands at your side if the word you hear does NOT start with the /f/ sound."

Word List: four, flowers, hand, fingers, ball, five, fork, spoon, friend, fish, fox, big, fan.

Ff

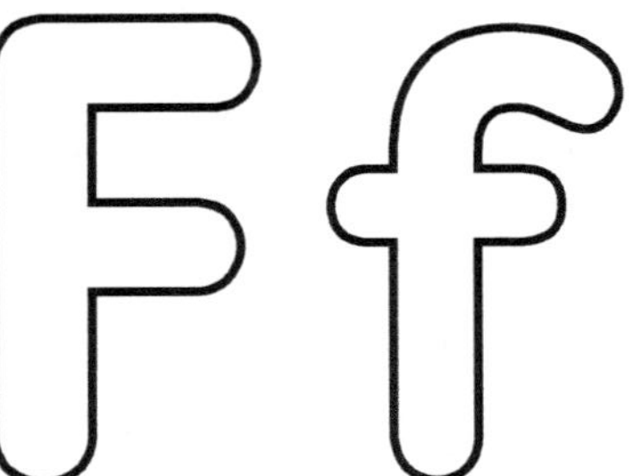

Page Instructions: Make your own "Ff" page. Draw or cut and paste pictures that start with the /f/ sound onto the page. Use the writing lines to practice letter shapes or copy simple sentences.

Activity: Play this game. Say, "Let's go around the room and everyone say a word that starts with the /f/ sound." Give additional clues if students are having difficulty.
Word List: fall, fan, fancy, farm, favorite, fence, finger, fire, first, fish, five, flag, flamingo, flashlight, flat, flower, fly, foot, football, forget, fork, four, friend, frog, full, funny, Friday, February, fun, fast, float.

Name ______________________________

Gg is for  .

Page Instructions: Help the student read, "G is for gumballs." Say, "Repeat the names of the pictures after me: gorilla with a guitar, girl, glue. What sound do you hear at the beginning of each word?" Tell the student to trace the letters in the boxes, start at the big dot. Color the page.

Activity: Play this game. Say, "I am going to say a word. Clap your hands if the word you hear starts with the /g/ sound. "
Word List: gorilla, good, game, banana, go, happy, green, grapes, grow, bear, girl.

Page Instructions: Make your own "Gg" page. Draw or cut and paste pictures that start with the /g/ sound onto the page. Use the writing lines to practice letter shapes or copy simple sentences.

Activity: Play this game. Say, "Let's go around the room and everyone say a word that starts with the /g/ sound." Give additional clues if students are having difficulty.

Word List: game, garbage, garden, gate, girl, glasses, gloves, glue, go, goat, goggles, gone, good, goose, gorilla, grandparents, grapes, graph, grasshopper, great, green, groundhog, guitar, gumballs, gray, give.

Name _______________

Hh is for

Page Instructions: Help the student read, "H is for helicopter." Say, "Repeat the names of the pictures after me: horse, heart, humming bird. What sound do you hear at the beginning of each word?" Tell the student to trace the letters in the boxes, start at the big dot. Color the page.

Activity: Play this game. Say, "I am going to say a word, listen carefully to it. If it starts with the /h/ sound, stand up! If it doesn't start with the /h/ sound, sit down."

Word List: happy, heavy, elephant, horn, house, girl, helicopter, hop, hug, big, hippo, boy, help, hot, cold, hungry, hundred.

Hh

Page Instructions: Make your own "Hh" page. Draw or cut and paste pictures that start with the /h/ sound onto the page. Use the writing lines to practice letter shapes or copy simple sentences.

Activity: Play this game. Say, "Let's go around the room and everyone say a word that starts with the /h/ sound." Give additional clues if students are having difficulty.

Word List: hair, half, hamburger, hammer, hand, happy, hat, head, heart, helicopter, hello, helmet, help, hi, hiccups, hill, hippo, hive, honey, hop, horn, horse, hose, hot, house, hug, humming bird, hundred, holiday, help.

Name ___________

Ii

is for

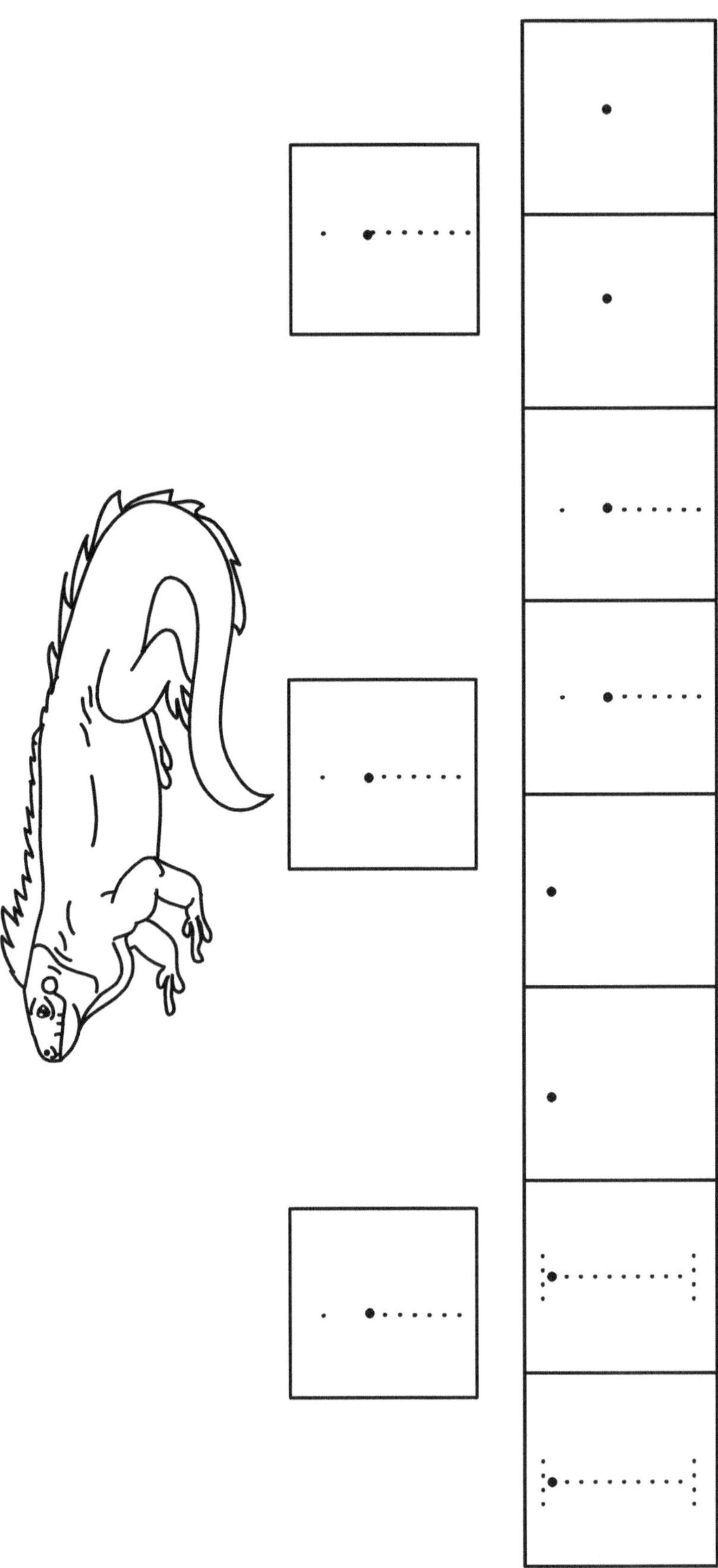

Page Instructions: Help the student read, "I is for igloo." Say, "Repeat the names of the pictures after me: igloo, iguana. What sound do you hear at the beginning of each word?" Tell the student to trace the letters in the boxes, start at the big dot. Color the page.

Activity: Play this game. Say, "I am going to say a word, listen carefully to it. If it starts with the /i/ sound, give me thumbs up! If it doesn't start with the /i/ sound, give me thumbs down."

Word List: igloo, turtle, inside, itchy, horse, ink, inch, camera, in, imagine, bed, incredible.

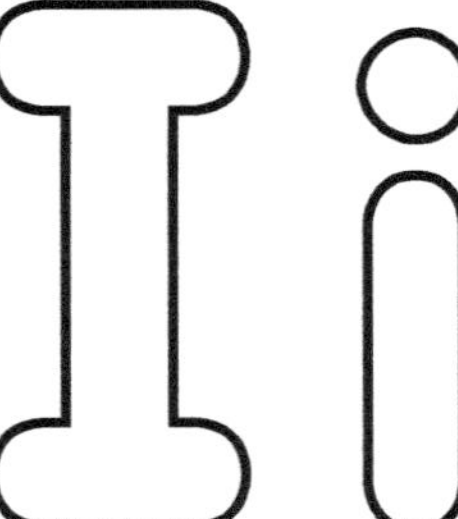

Page Instructions: Make your own "Ii" page. Draw, cut and paste pictures that start with the /i/ sound. Cut and paste words with the letter I from magazines or newspapers. Use the lines to practice writing letters and/or copy simple words & sentences.

Activity: Make three boxes on the board. Write the short vowel in the middle box. Add beginning and ending consonants such as "b" and "g." Track as you segment and blend the word: /b/-/i/-/g/, /big/. Say, "Let's think of more words that have /i/ in the middle, like BIG." Give additional clues if students are having difficulty.
Word List: chin, chick, did, dig, dish, drip, fin, fish, fix, flip, hill, him, his, hit, kick, kid, kiss, lick, lid, lip, milk, miss, mitt, mix, pick, pig, pin, pink, ribs, rip, ship, sink, sit, six, swim, tick, tip, trick, trip, wig, will, win, wink, wish, zip.

Name ____________________

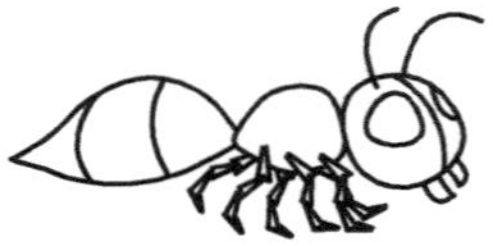 i 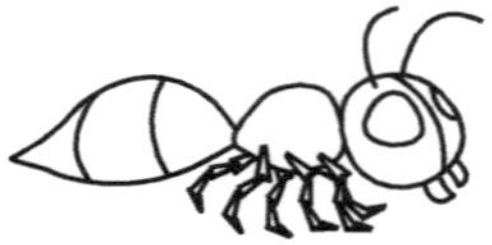 i

I i I i

I 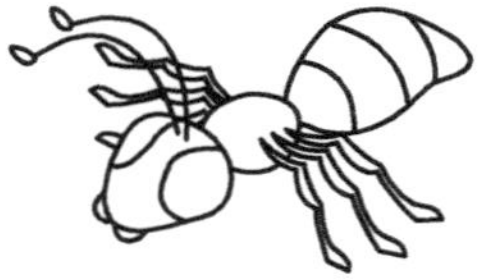 I 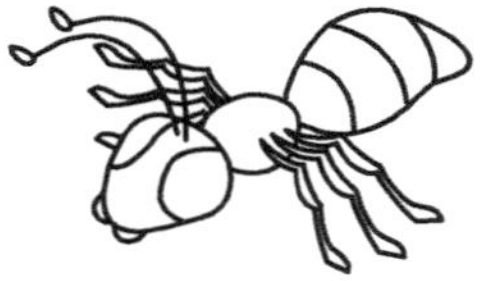

Page Instructions: Look at the first row, start at the left. Try to complete the pattern by filling in the dotted boxes. Try the same technique on the second and third row. Use the blank space at the bottom to make your own pattern!

Name

My Insect

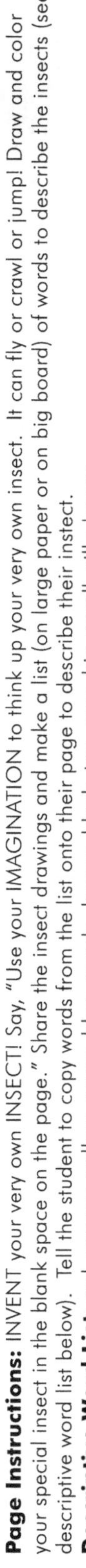

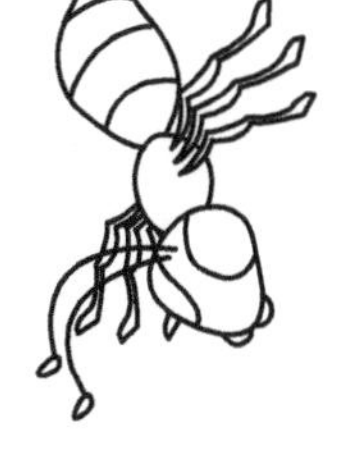

Page Instructions: INVENT your very very own insect. It can fly or crawl or jump! Draw and color your special insect in the blank space on the page. Say, "Use your IMAGINATION to think up your very own INSECT! Share the insect drawings and make a list (on large paper or on big board) of words to describe the insects (see descriptive word list below). Tell the student to copy words from the list onto their page to describe their instect.

Descriptive Word List: red, orange, yellow, green, blue, purple, brown, black, tan, grey, big, small, silly, happy.

Name _______________

Jj

Jj is for

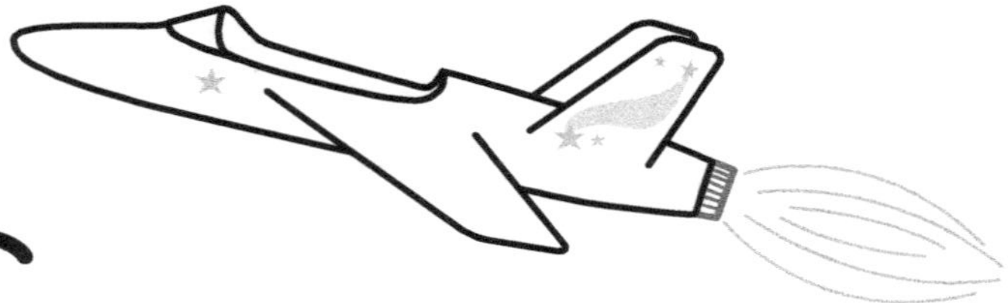

Page Instructions: Help the student read, "J is for jet." Say, "Repeat the names of the pictures after me: juggler, jumprope, jeep. What sound do you hear at the beginning of each word?" Tell the student to trace the letters in the boxes, start at the big dot. Color the page.

Activity: Play this game. Line up students at the back of the room. Say, "I am going to say a word. Take one jump forward if the word you hear starts with the /j/ sound."

Word List: jar, jam, toast, jeans, shirt, jacket, jewelry, hat, juice, milk, jungle, jaguar, cat, jeep.

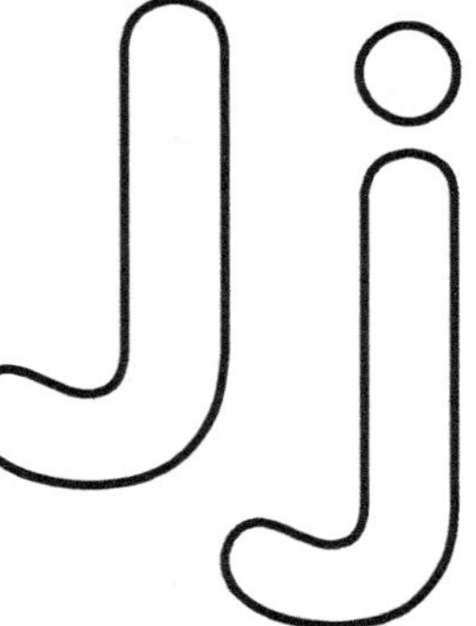

Page Instructions: Make your own "Jj" page. Draw or cut and paste pictures that start with the /j/ sound onto the page. Use the writing lines to practice letter shapes or copy simple sentences.

Activity: Play this game. Say, "Let's go around the room and everyone say a word that starts with the /j/ sound." Give additional clues if students are having difficulty.

Word List: jacks, jacket, jaguar, jam, jar, jeans, jeep, jelly, jellybeans, jet, jewelry, jingle, job, jog, jogging, jolly, journey, jug, juggle, juggler, juice, jump, jumprope, jungle, January, June, July.

Name

Kk is for

Page Instructions: Help the student read, "K is for kite." Say, "Repeat the names of the pictures after me: king, keys, kangaroo. What sound do you hear at the beginning of each word?" Tell the student to trace the letters in the boxes, start at the big dot. Color the page.

Activity: Play this game. Be sure each student has a YES and NO card. Say, "I am going to say a word. If you think the word starts with the /k/ sound, hold up your YES card. If you think the word does NOT start with the /k/ sound, hold up your NO card."

Word List: kite, kindergarten, girl, kiss, kitchen, jet, kids, ketchup, hair, kind, apple, keys.

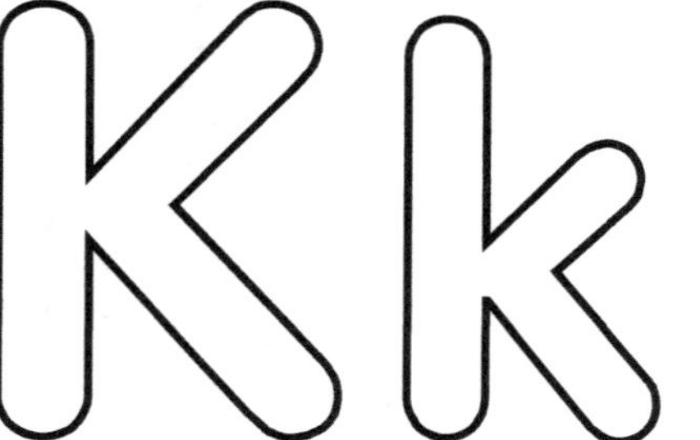

Page Instructions: Make your own "Kk" page. Draw or cut and paste pictures that start with the /k/ sound onto the page. Use the writing lines to practice letter shapes or copy simple sentences.

Activity: Play this game. Say, "Let's go around the room and everyone say a word that starts with the /k/ sound." Give additional clues if students are having difficulty.
Word List: kangaroo, keep, ketchup, key, keyboard, kick, kids, kind, kindergarten, king, kiss, kitchen, kite, kitten, koala, kit, kimono, kilt, kidney, kettle, kernel, kayak, kelp, kaleidoscope, kiwi.

Name ___________________________

Ll

is for 

Page Instructions: Help the student read, "L is for lips." Say, "Repeat the names of the pictures after me: log, lock, licking the lollipop. What sound do you hear at the beginning of each word?" Tell the student to trace the letters in the boxes, start at the big dot. Color the page.

Activity: Play this game. Say, "I am going to say a word. Put your hands on your head if the word you hear starts with the /l/ sound. Keep your hands at your side if the word you hear does NOT start with the /l/ sound."

Word List: lollipop, lick, jelly, lemon, little, big, love, good, lightning, leaf, tree, lamp.

Ll

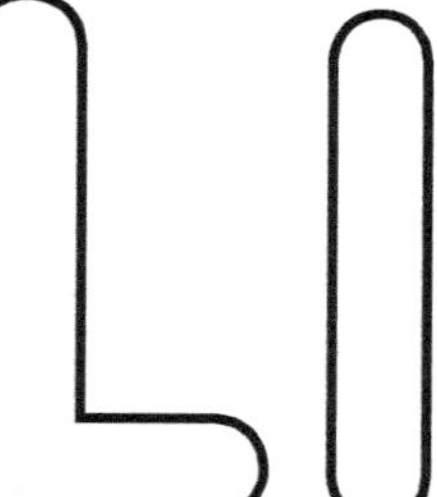

Page Instructions: Make your own "Ll" page. Draw or cut and paste pictures that start with the /l/ sound onto the page. Use the writing lines to practice letter shapes or copy simple sentences.

Activity: Play this game. Say, "Let's go around the room and everyone say a word that starts with the /l/ sound." Give additional clues if students are having difficulty.

Word List: ladder, ladybug, lamp, large, last, leaf, lemon, lettuce, library, lick, light, like, line, lion, lips, little, lizard, lobster, lock, log, lollipop, look, lots, love, lucky, lightning, left, leg, lake.

Name

Mm

Mm is for ___ .

Page Instructions: Help the student read, "M is for monkey." Say, "Repeat the names of the pictures after me: mask, motorcycle, moon. What sound do you hear at the beginning of each word?" Tell the student to trace the letters in the boxes, start at the big dot. Color the page.

Activity: Play this game. Say, "I am going to say a word. Clap your hands if the word you hear starts with the /m/ sound."

Word List: milk, mermaid, monster, happy, me, marbles, dad, mom, mouse, house, music.

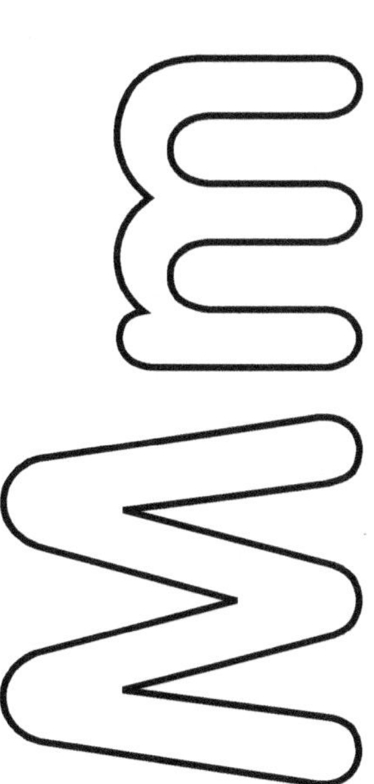

Page Instructions: Make your own "Mm" page. Draw or cut and paste pictures that start with the /m/ sound onto the page. Use the writing lines to practice letter shapes or copy simple sentences.

Activity: Play this game. Say, "Let's go around the room and everyone say a word that starts with the /m/ sound." Give additional clues if students are having difficulty.

Word List: mountain, magic, mail, make, man, map, marbles, marvelous, mask, maze, me, memory, mermaid, milk, mirror, mittens, mix, mole, mom, monkey, monster, moon, moose, mop, morning, movie, music.

Name _______________________

Nn is for 9.

Page Instructions: Help the student read, "N is for number nine." Say, "Repeat the names of the pictures after me: note, net, nest. What sound do you hear at the beginning of each word?" Tell the student to trace the letters in the boxes, start at the big dot. Color the page.

Activity: Play this game. Say, "I am going to say a word, listen carefully to it. If it starts with the /n/ sound, give me thumbs up! If it doesn't start with the /n/ sound, give me thumbs down."

Word List: nine, net, bird, nice, note, pen, nap, cat, nose, number, day, night, plant, nature.

Page Instructions: Make your own "Nn" page. Draw or cut and paste pictures that start with the /n/ sound onto the page. Use the writing lines to practice letter shapes or copy simple sentences.

Activity: Play this game. Say, "Let's go around the room and everyone say a word that starts with the /n/ sound." Give additional clues if students are having difficulty.

Word List: nail, name, nap, nature, near, necklace, nest, net, new, newspaper, next, nice, nickel, night, nine, no, noise, none, noodles, north, nose, note, notebook, now, numbers, nurse, nuts, never, November.

Name ___________

Page Instructions: Help the student read, "O is for octopus." Say, "Repeat the names of the pictures after me: on, ostrich, off. What sound do you hear at the beginning of each word?" Tell the student to trace the letters in the boxes, start at the big dot. Color the page.

Activity: Play this game. Say, "I am going to say a word. Put your hands on your head if the word you hear starts with the /o/ sound. Keep your hands at your side if the word you hear does NOT start with the /o/ sound."

Word List: on, off, green, octopus, friend, October, pumpkin, opposite, ox, car, olive.

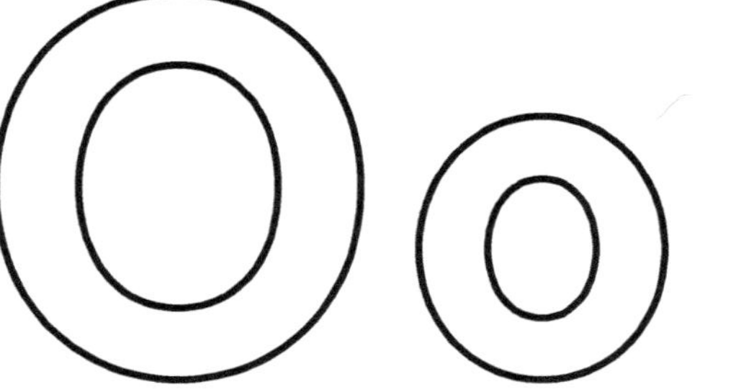

Page Instructions: Make your own "Oo" page. Draw, cut and paste pictures that start with the /o/ sound. Cut and paste words with the letter O from magazines or newspapers. Use the lines to practice writing letters and/or copy simple words & sentences.

Activity: Make three boxes on the board. Write the short vowel in the middle box. Add beginning and ending consonants such as "f" and "x." Track as you segment and blend the word: /f/-/o/-/x/, /fox/. Say, "Let's think of more words that have /o/ in the middle, like FOX." Give additional clues if students are having difficulty.

Word List: box, clock, doll, dog, dot, drop, fog, frog, got, hog, hop, hot, job, jog, knot, lock, log, lots, mom, mop, nod, not, pond, pop, pot, rock, shop, sock, spot, stop, tock, top.

Name ____

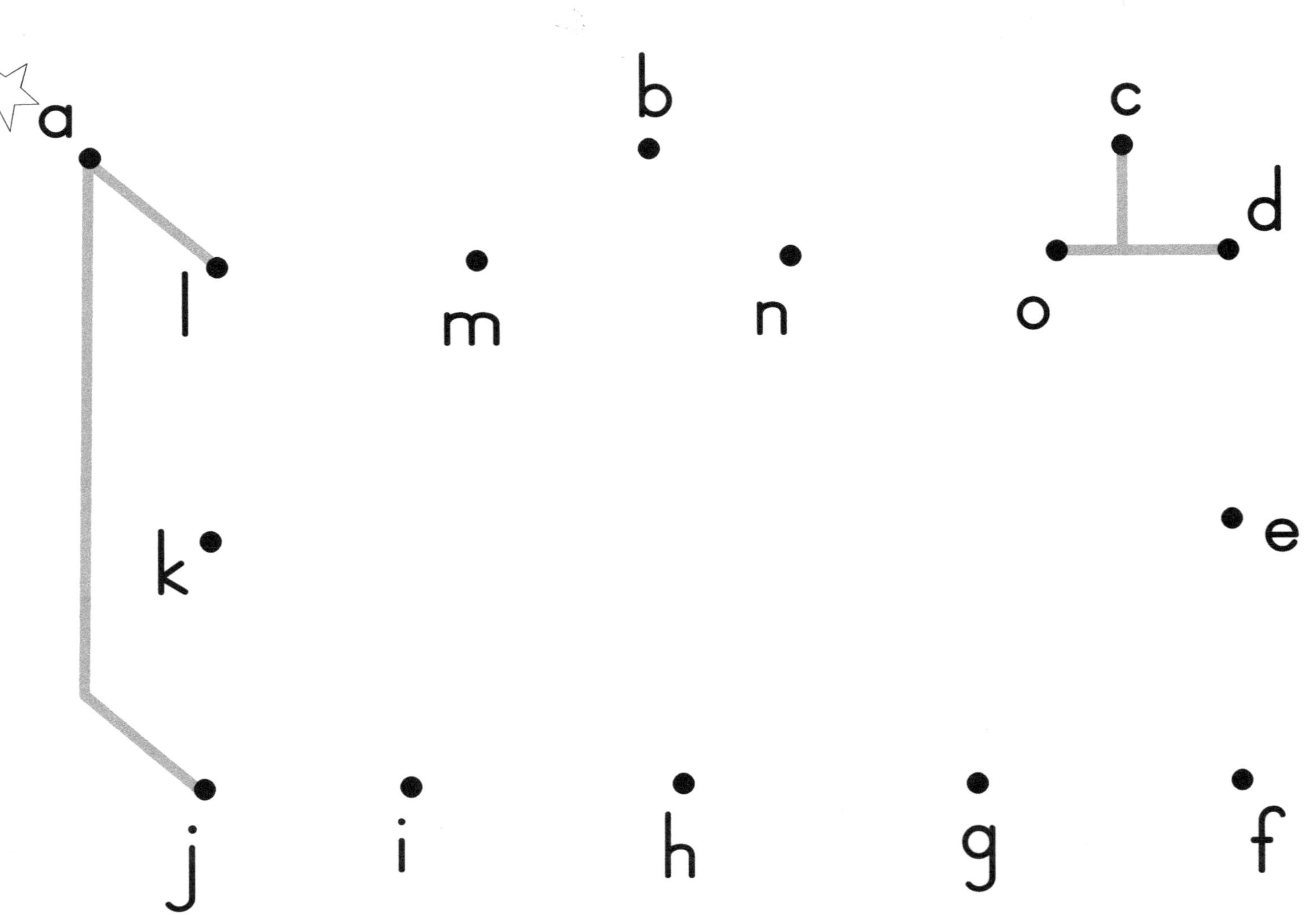

Page Instructions: Follow the dots in alphabetical order, lower-case A to O and see what you find! Use the star to help students locate the starting point: letter a.

Activity: Make three boxes on the board. Write the short vowel in the middle box. Add beginning and ending consonants "b" and "x". Track as you segment and blend the word: /b/-/o/-/x/, /box/. Ask the students to copy the word "box" somewhere on their page. Ask the students to color and decorate their page and draw things in the box. Let the students share what they drew in their boxes with the class.

Name

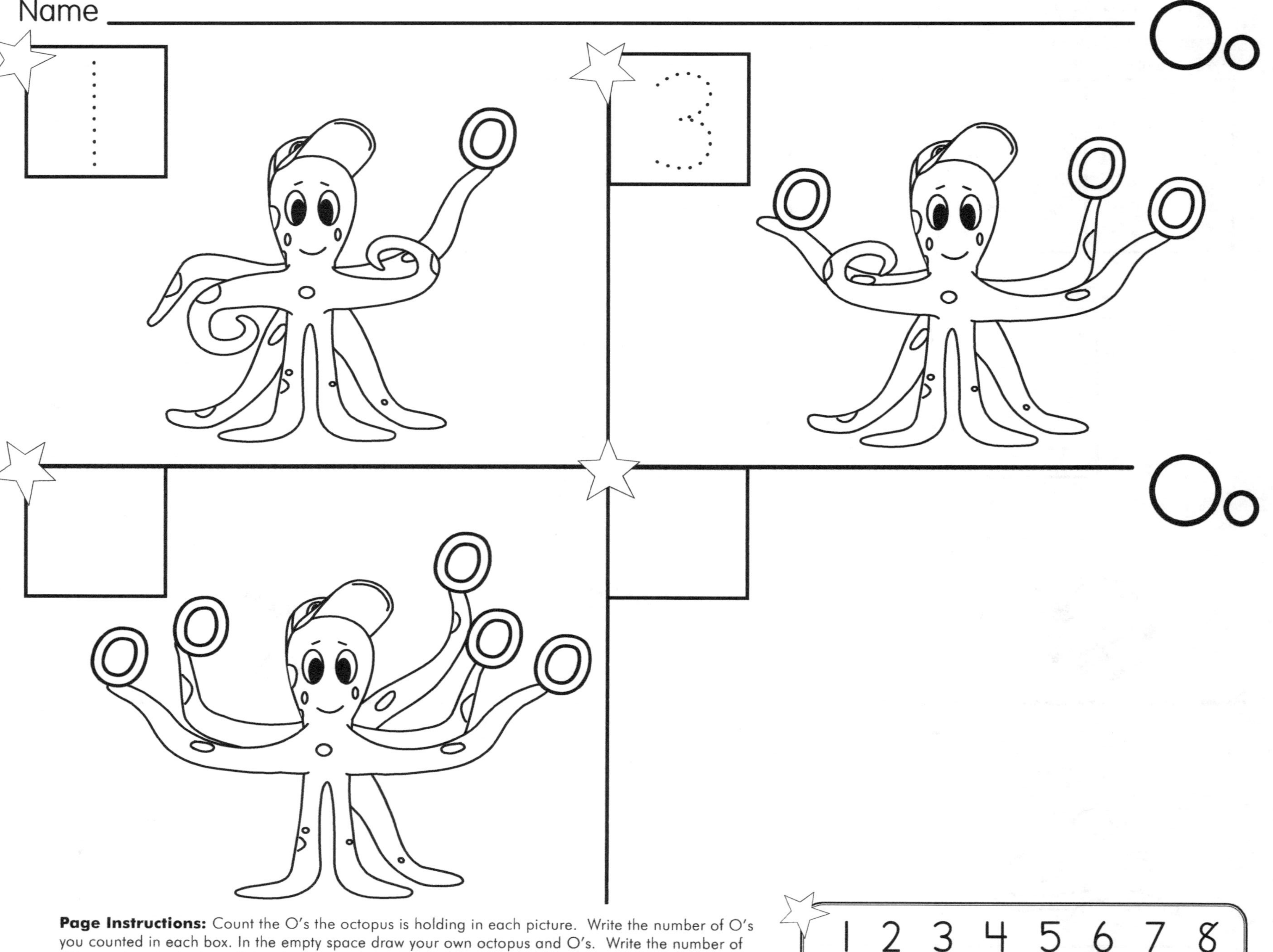

1 2 3 4 5 6 7 8

Page Instructions: Count the O's the octopus is holding in each picture. Write the number of O's you counted in each box. In the empty space draw your own octopus and O's. Write the number of O's you drew in the box. Color the page.

Name _______________________

Pp is for  .

Page Instructions: Help the student read, "P is for pizza." Say, "Repeat the names of the pictures after me: push, pumpkin, pull. What sound do you hear at the beginning of each word?" Tell the student to trace the letters in the boxes, start at the big dot. Color the page.

Activity: Play this game. Say, "I am going to say a word, listen carefully to it. If it starts with the /p/ sound, stand up! If it doesn't start with the /p/ sound, sit down."

Word List: paint, pancakes, syrup, paper, pencil, water, pillow, popcorn, pizza, candy, pepperoni, noodles, puzzle, puppet, nose, penguin, cold, picture, pig, nuts, parrot.

Page Instructions: Make your own "Pp" page. Draw or cut and paste pictures that start with the /p/ sound onto the page. Use the writing lines to practice letter shapes or copy simple sentences.

Activity: Play this game. Say, "Let's go around the room and everyone say a word that starts with the /p/ sound." Give additional clues if students are having difficulty.

Word List: package, paint, pajamas, pancake, paper, parents, parrot, peacock, penguin, pepperoni, penny, pickle, picture, pie, pig, pillow, pin, pizza, plane, planet, poodle, popcorn, popsicle, presents, pretty, pull, push.

Name ___________________________

Qq is for ?.

Page Instructions: Help the student read, "Q is for question." Say, "Repeat the names of the pictures after me: quilt, question mark, queen. What sound do you hear at the beginning of each word?" Tell the student to trace the letters in the boxes, start at the big dot. Color the page.

Activity: Play this game. Be sure each student has a YES and NO card. Say, "I am going to say a word. If you think the word starts with the /kw/ sound, hold up your YES card. If you think the word does NOT start with the /kw/ sound, hold up your NO card."

Word List: quilt, question, baby, quarter, dog, quick, quiet, bear, quack, duck, quail, queen.

Qq

Page Instructions: Make your own "Qq" page. Draw, cut and paste pictures that start with the /kw/ sound. Cut and paste words with the letter Q from magazines or newspapers. Use the lines to practice writing letters and/or copy simple words & sentences.

Activity: Play this game. Say, "Let's go around the room and everyone say a word that starts with the /kw/ sound." Give additional clues if students are having difficulty.

Word List: quack, quail, quarter, queen, quench, question, quick, quickly, quiet, quilt, quit, quiver.

Name _______________________

Rr is for ___________ .

Page Instructions: Help the student read, "R is for rain." Say, "Repeat the names of the pictures after me: rainbow, rope, rose. What sound do you hear at the beginning of each word?" Tell the student to trace the letters in the boxes, start at the big dot. Color the page.

Activity: Play this game. Line up students at the back of the room. Say, "I am going to say a word. Take one step forward if the word you hear starts with the /r/ sound."
Word List: robot, red, pencil, radio, raccoon, nickel, round, right, left, lunch, juice, rope.

Rr

Page Instructions: Make your own "Rr" page. Draw or cut and paste pictures that start with the /r/ sound onto the page. Use the writing lines to practice letter shapes or copy simple sentences.

Activity: Play this game. Say, "Let's go around the room and everyone say a word that starts with the /r/ sound." Give additional clues if students are having difficulty.

Word List: rabbit, raccoon, radio, rain, rainbow, rake, rat, rattle, rectangle, red, refrigerator, remember, rhino, ridiculous, ring, river, robot, rocket, roll, roof, rooster, rope, rose, round, rug, ruler, right, race.

Name ___________________________________

Ss is for S.

Page Instructions: Help the student read, "S is for snake." Say, "Repeat the names of the pictures after me: sun, skateboard, star. What sound do you hear at the beginning of each word?" Tell the student to trace the letters in the boxes, start at the big dot. Color the page.

Activity: Play this game. Say, "I am going to say a word. Clap your hands if the word you hear starts with the /s/ sound. "
Word List: six, seven, five, socks, sandwich, red, summer, race, sleep, sun, parrot, sing.

Ss

Page Instructions: Make your own "Ss" page. Draw or cut and paste pictures that start with the /s/ sound onto the page. Use the writing lines to practice letter shapes or copy simple sentences.

Activity: Play this game. Say, "Let's go around the room and everyone say a word that starts with the /s/ sound." Give additional clues if students are having difficulty.

Word List: saddle, sail, salad, sand, sandwich, scary, seal, sea, secret, seesaw, seven, sit, six, skateboard, sleep, snake, sock, space, stars, stick, stop, stretch, summer, sun, square, sing, September, Saturday, Sunday, sign, soft.

Name _______________________

T t is for ____________ .

10

Page Instructions: Help the student read, "T is for tiger." Say, "Repeat the names of the pictures after me: taxi, ten, train. What sound do you hear at the beginning of each word?" Tell the student to trace the letters in the boxes, start at the big dot. Color the page.

Activity: Play this game. Say, "I am going to say a word, listen carefully to it. If it starts with the /t/ sound, give me thumbs up! If it doesn't start with the /t/ sound, give me thumbs down."
Word List: train, tiger, snake, two, four, teeth, toys, box, tree, leaf, Tuesday, ten, sand, turkey.

Tt

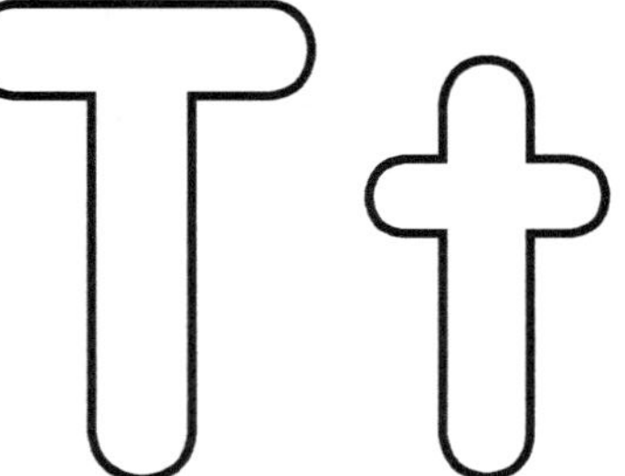

Page Instructions: Make your own "Tt" page. Draw or cut and paste pictures that start with the /t/ sound onto the page. Use the writing lines to practice letter shapes or copy simple sentences.

Activity: Play this game. Say, "Let's go around the room and everyone say a word that starts with the /t/ sound." Give additional clues if students are having difficulty.

Word List: table, tail, tall, tape, taxi, tea, teeth, telephone, television, ten, tie, tiger, tomato, tongue, tooth, top, toys, tractor, trail, train, treasure, tree, triangle, trucks, trunk, tub, turkey, turtle, twins, two, Tuesday.

Name ______________________________

Uu is for  .

Page Instructions: Help the student read, "U is for umbrella." Say, "Repeat the names of the pictures after me: umbrella, under the umbrella, upside-down umbrella. What sound do you hear at the beginning of each word?" Tell the student to trace the letters in the boxes, start at the big dot. Color the page.

Activity: Play this game. Say, "I am going to say a word. Clap your hands if the word you hear starts with the /u/ sound. "
Word List: up, under, down, umbrella, rain, uncle, underground, moon, umpire, baseball, underline, pencil, unfold, paper, unlock, uphill, me, us.

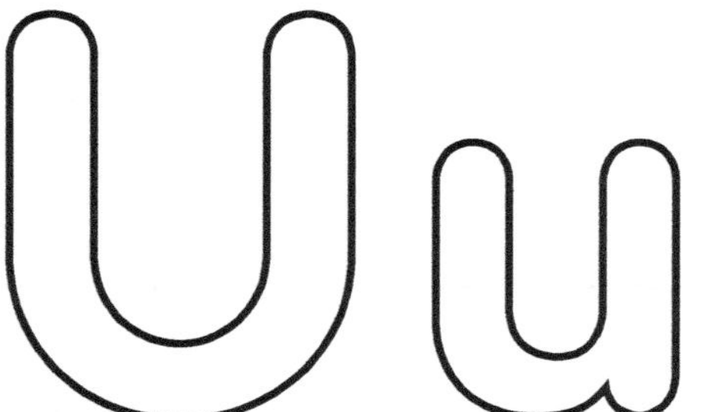

Page Instructions: Make your own "Uu" page. Draw, cut and paste pictures that start with the /u/ sound. Cut and paste words with the letter U from magazines or newspapers. Use the lines to practice writing letters and/or copy simple words & sentences.

Activity: Make three boxes on the board. Write the short vowel in the middle box. Add beginning and ending consonants such as "f" and "n." Track as you segment and blend the word: /f/-/u/-/n/, /fun/. Say, "Let's think of more words that have /u/ in the middle, like FUN." Give additional clues if students are having difficulty.

Word List: brush, bun, bus, but, club, cub, cup, cut, drum, duck, dug, dust, fuzz, fun, hug, hum, hunt, hut, jump, just, luck, lump, mud, mug, nut, plug, plum, plus, pup, rub, rug, rush, sub, suds, sun, truck, trunk, tub, tug.

Name _______________________________

Page Instructions: Tell the student to trace the letters in the boxes. Start at the big dot and trace each letter with a pencil. Read the words with the student one at a time. Ask the student to draw a line from the word to the correct picture. Start by tracing the example line from the word "tub" to the picture. Color the page.

Name ______________________________

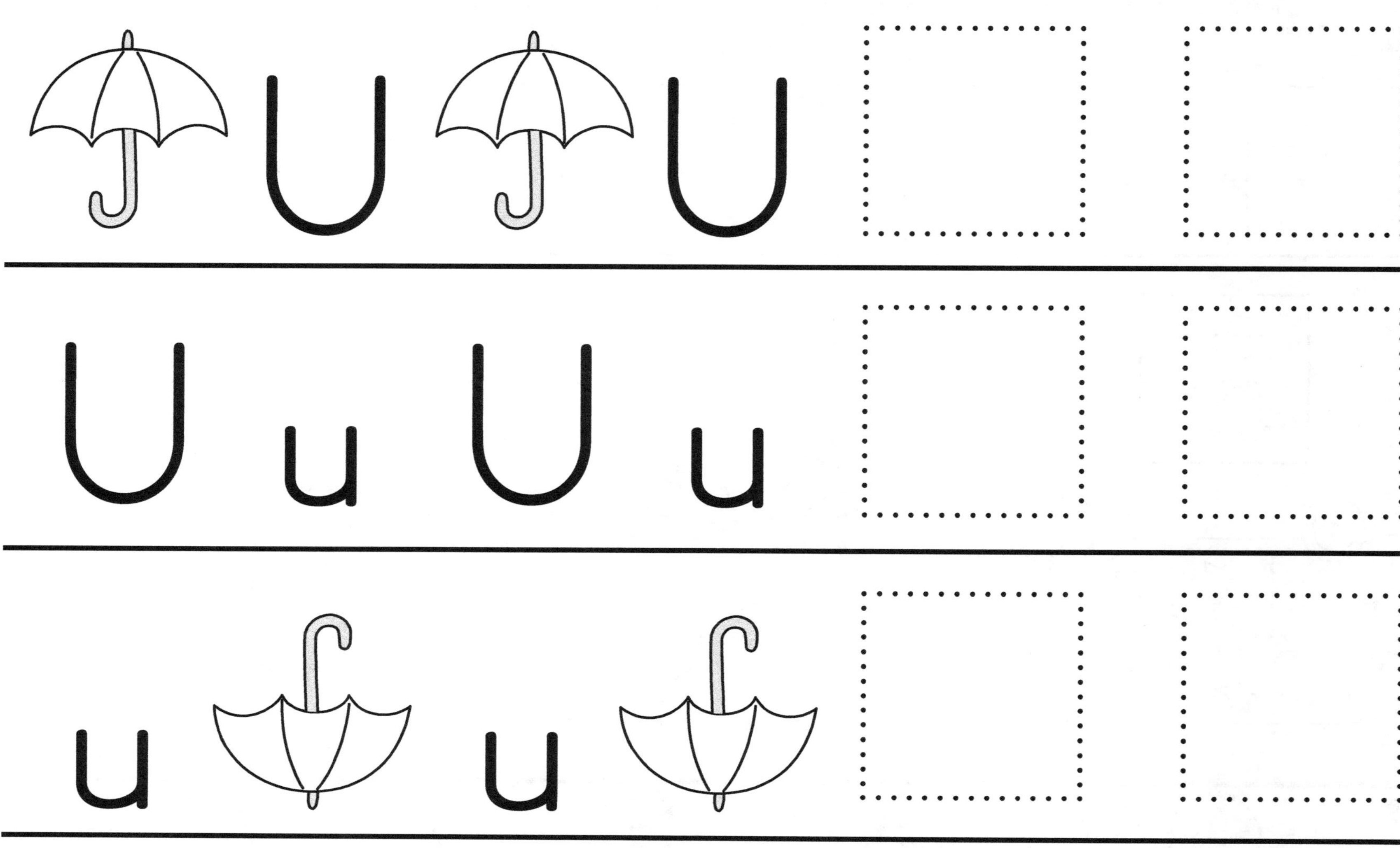

Page Instructions: Look at the first row, start at the left. Try to complete the pattern by filling in the dotted boxes. Try the same technique on the second and third row. Use the blank space at the bottom to make your own pattern!

Name _______________

Vv is for _______ .

Page Instructions: Help the student read, "V is for violin." Say, "Repeat the names of the pictures after me: vacuum, volcano, van. What sound do you hear at the beginning of each word?" Tell the student to trace the letters in the boxes, start at the big dot. Color the page.

Activity: Play this game. Be sure each student has a YES and NO card. Say, "I am going to say a word. If you think the word starts with the /v/ sound, hold up your YES card. If you think the word does NOT start with the /v/ sound, hold up your NO card."

Word List: vegetables, vanilla, chocolate, vase, flower, visit, volcano, moon, valley, vine.

Page Instructions: Make your own "Vv" page. Draw or cut and paste pictures that start with the /v/ sound onto the page. Use the writing lines to practice letter shapes or copy simple sentences.

Activity: Play this game. Say, "Let's go around the room and everyone say a word that starts with the /v/ sound." Give additional clues if students are having difficulty.

Word List: vacuum, valentine, valley, van, vanilla, vase, vegetables, very, vest, video, vine, violin, visit, visor, volcano, vowels, violet, voice.

Name ___________

Ww is for

Page Instructions: Help the student read, "W is for window." Say, "Repeat the names of the pictures after me: wolf, wig, web. What sound do you hear at the beginning of each word?" Tell the student to trace the letters in the boxes, start at the big dot. Color the page.

Activity: Play this game. Say, "I am going to say a word. Put your hands on your head if the word you hear starts with the /w/ sound. Keep your hands at your side if the word you hear does NOT start with the /w/ sound."

Word List: water, wet, rain, waves, surf, windy, winter, snow, worm, dirt, Wednesday.

Page Instructions: Make your own "Ww" page. Draw or cut and paste pictures that start with the /w/ sound onto the page. Use the writing lines to practice letter shapes or copy simple sentences.

Activity: Play this game. Say, "Let's go around the room and everyone say a word that starts with the /w/ sound." Give additional clues if students are having difficulty.

Word List: wagon, walrus, warm, watch, water, watermelon, waterfall, waves, weather, web, welcome, wet, whale, wheel, whistle, wide, wig, window, windy, winter, wishing well, wolf, word, world, worm, Wednesday.

Name _______

Xx

X is in six.

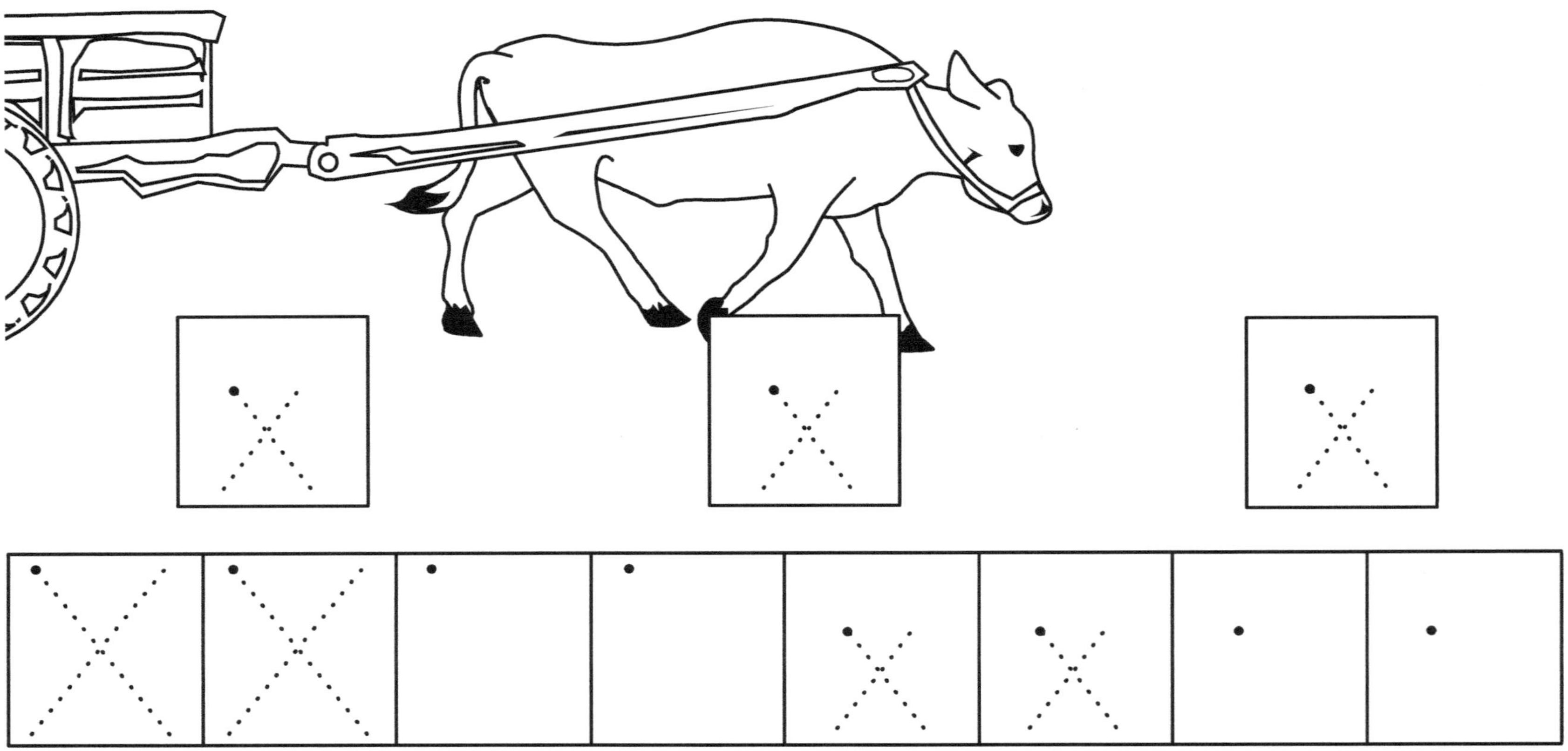

Page Instructions: Help the student read, "X is in six." Say, "Repeat the names of the pictures after me: six, ox. What sound do you hear at the end of each word?" Tell the student to trace the letters in the boxes, start at the big dot. Color the page.

Activity: Make the shape of the letter X with your body! Stand up and make a big X with your arms in the air and your legs wide apart. Make little x's with your fingers. Cross your wrists, then your elbows to make X's with your arms. Find other things in the shape of X. Have fun!

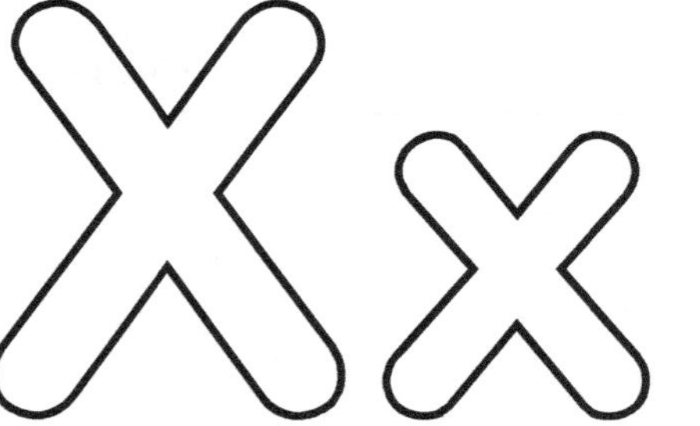

Page Instructions: Make your own "Xx" page. Draw or cut and paste pictures that look like X OR that start or end with the /ks/ sound. Cut and paste words with the letter X from magazines or newspapers. Use the writing lines to practice letter shapes or copy simple sentences.

Activity: Play tic tac toe with X's and O's. Play on a big board or paper, let students take turns being X or O. Go over a few words that have the /ks/ sound in between games. Talk about where you hear the /ks/ sound, at the beginning, middle or end of each word.

Word List: box, excellent, excited, exciting, exit, extra, extremely, fox, six, x-ray, extra, mix, T-rex, ox.

Name _______________________

Yy is for

Page Instructions: Help the student read, "Y is for yo-yo." Say, "Repeat the names of the pictures after me: yo-yo, yodel. What sound do you hear at the beginning of each word?" Tell the student to trace the letters in the boxes, start at the big dot. Color the page.

Activity: Play this game. Line up students at the back of the room. Say, "I am going to say a word. Take one step forward if the word you hear starts with the /y/ sound."
Word List: yak, yellow, up, yawn, yesterday, tomorrow, you, me, yell, talk, young, yippee!

Yy

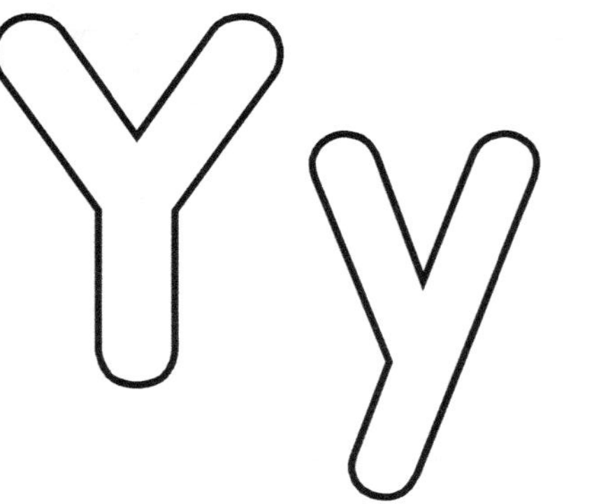

Page Instructions: Make your very own "Yy" page. Draw or cut and paste pictures that start with the /y/ sound onto the page. Cut and paste words with the letter Y from magazines or newspapers. Use the writing lines to practice letter shapes or copy simple sentences.

Activity: Play this game. Say, "Let's go around the room and everyone say a word that starts with the /y/ sound." Give additional clues if students are having difficulty.
Word List: yak, yarn, yawn, yellow, yes, yesterday, yippee, you, young, yo-yo, yell, yams, yard, yeast, year, yoga, yolk, yield, yourself.

Name _______________

Zz is for ____.

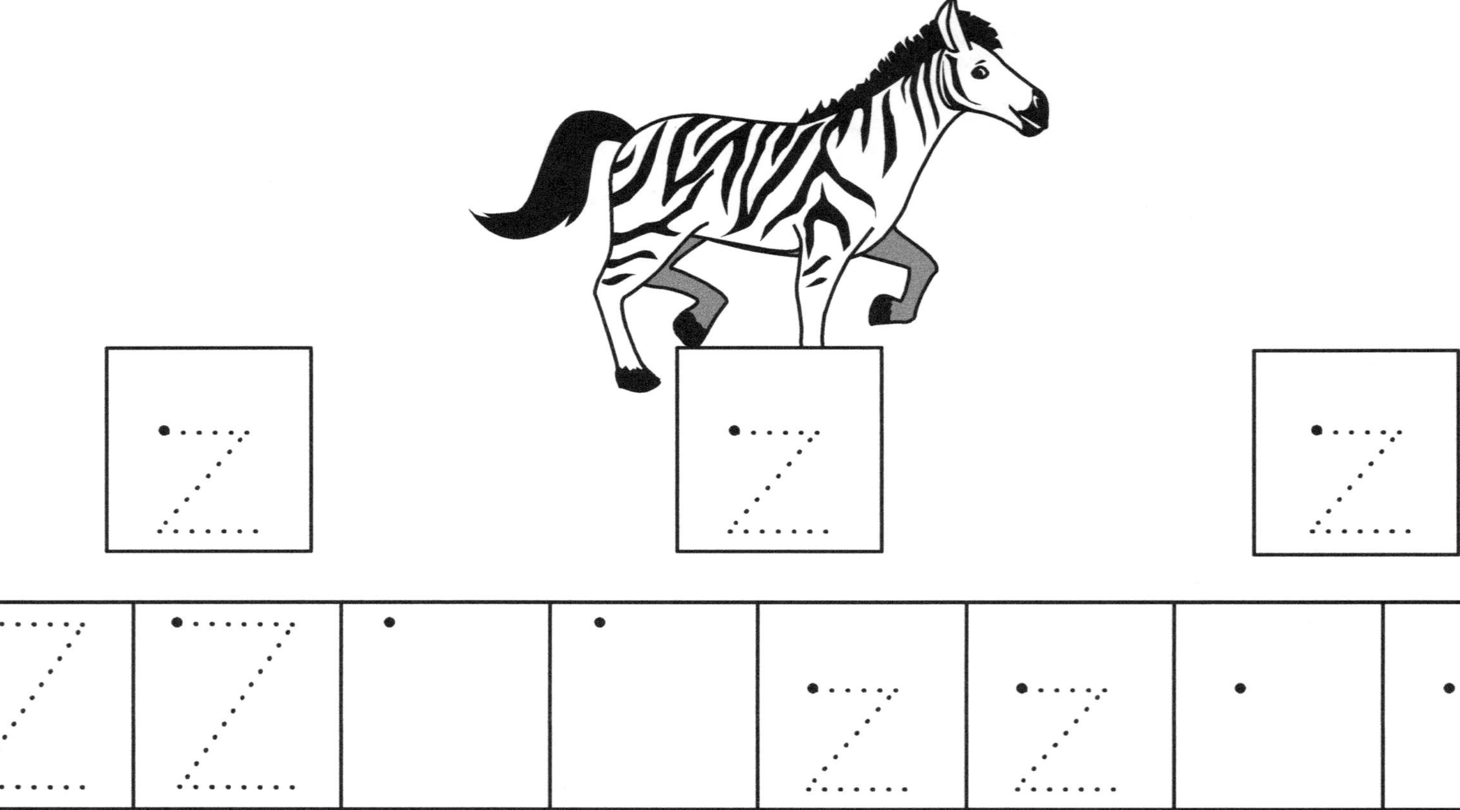

Page Instructions: Help the student read, "Z is for zipper." Say, "Repeat the names of the pictures after me: zipper, zebra. What sound do you hear at the beginning of each word?" Tell the student to trace the letters in the boxes, start at the big dot. Tell the student the zebra is at the ZOO. Draw more animals at the zoo & color the page.

Activity: Play this game. Say, "I am going to say a word. Clap your hands if the word you hear starts with the /z/ sound. "
Word List: zoo, zebra, monkey, zero, two, zip, buttons, jacket, zone, blue, zig-zag.

Zz

Page Instructions: Make your own "Zz" page. Draw or cut and paste pictures that start with the /z/ sound onto the page. Cut and paste words with the letter Z from magazines or newspapers. Use the writing lines to practice letter shapes or copy simple sentences.

Activity: Play this game. Say, "Let's go around the room and I'll say a word that has the /z/ sound in it. Tell me where the /z/ sound is, in the beginning, in the middle or at the end of the word."

Word List: zag, breeze, zap, blizzard, zebra, buzz, zero, buzzard, daze, dozen, zest, zinc, freeze, fizz, frozen, zipper, fuzz, hazy, zone, prize, zonk, size, sneeze, squeeze, zoo, zoom, snooze, whiz.

Name ______________________________

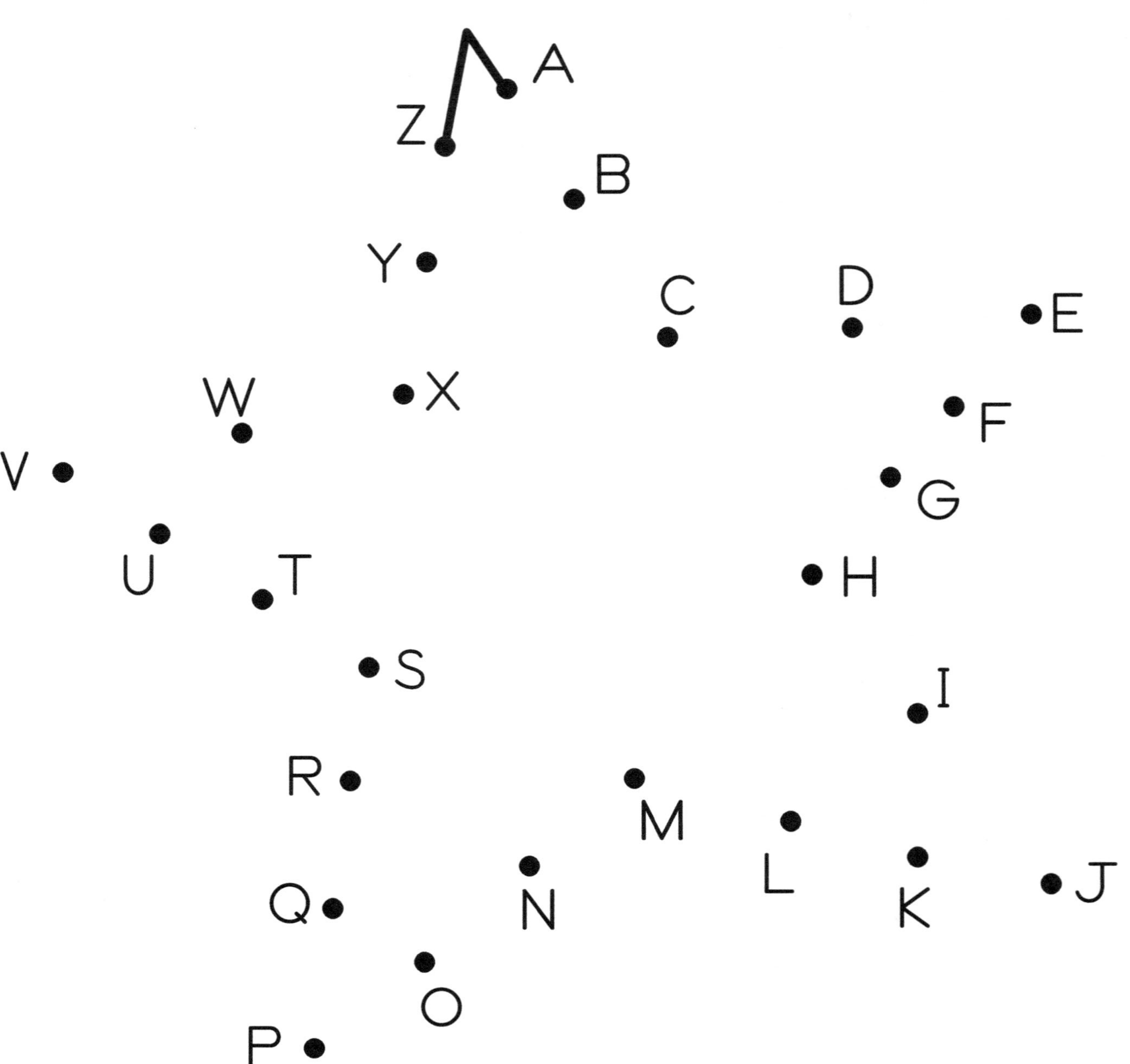

Name ______________________________

See the big fish. 

3
4
5

I am a little girl.

3
4
5

Look at the moon.

3
4
5

I like to eat pizza.

3
4
5

Page Instructions: Count the number of words in each sentence and circle the correct number. Circle the word in the sentence that names each picture. Color the pictures.

DADAM*trace*©

Copyright © 2020 by DADAM*trace* **©**